AN INTRODUCTION TO EDGAR CAYCE

Here for the first time is a popularly written book presenting a simplified approach to the issues and philosophy underpinning the Edgar Cayce readings in the psychic area. DR. HERBERT B. PURYEAR, an acknowledged authority on Cayce's work, is Director of Research Services for the Association for Research and Enlightenment (A.R.E.) in Virginia Beach, Virginia.

Dr. Puryear is author of *Reflections on the Path* and coauthor of *Meditations and the Mind of Man.* He is also author of the A.R.E. membership lesson series, *Covenant,* upon which much of *The Edgar Cayce Primer* is based. Several years ago, Dr. Puryear hosted a nationally televised, twenty-six part series, *Who Is Man?,* an extensive inquiry into parapsychological research.

A trained clinical psychologist, Dr. Puryear received his Ph.D. from the University of North Carolina, and his B.A. from Stanford University.

D0802036

Bantam Books of Related Interest

THE EDGAR CAYCE PRIMER by Herbert Bruce Puryear, Ph.D.
EDGAR CAYCE: THE SLEEPING PROPHET by Jess Stearn

THE
EDGAR CAYCE
PRIMER

Herbert B. Puryear

Edited by Richard I. Abrams

BANTAM BOOKS
TORONTO · NEW YORK · LONDON · SYDNEY

THE EDGAR CAYCE PRIMER

A Bantam Book / September 1982

ISBN 0-553-22738-6

Published simultaneously in the United States and Canada

Bantam Books are published by Bantam Books, Inc. Its
trademark, consisting of the words "Bantam Books" and
the portrayal of a rooster, is Registered in U.S. Patent and
Trademark Office and in other countries. Marca Registrada.
Bantam Books, Inc., 666 Fifth Avenue, New York, New
York 10103.

PRINTED IN THE UNITED STATES OF AMERICA

O   0 9 8 7 6 5 4 3 2 1

ACKNOWLEDGMENTS

Many books are the product of intensive research and writing over a period of months. However, this book is the result of much cumulative experience over several decades. For this reason I wish to use this opportunity to acknowledge some of the special contributions others have made to my life, enabling me to write this particular kind of book.

The Edgar Cayce story was introduced to me in 1951 by my fiancée, Meredith Ann, who in the same year became my wife. She opened the door for a marvelous new direction in my life—the opportunity to study the Edgar Cayce readings. For this I continue to be grateful.

We first visited Virginia Beach in 1953. Here we met Mae Gimbert St. Clair and Gladys Davis Turner, members of the Association for Research and Enlightenment staff, who through the years and in very special ways made the Edgar Cayce readings available and understandable for us. At that time we also met Hugh Lynn Cayce, who became and has continued to be a great source of inspiration and motivation. It was he who enabled us in 1969 to move into this area of study, making it a life work.

For my understanding of the Bible I owe much to my high school pastor, J. Ralph Grant. For introducing and encouraging me in the scientific study of parapsychology I am grateful to J. B. Rhine of Duke University. For my appreciation of the comparative study of religions I am thankful for the work of Freidrich Spieglberg of Stanford University.

My opportunities to become a psychologist were especially enhanced by Leland Winder of Stanford University, Earl Baughman and Grant Dahlstrom of the University of North Carolina, and Kenneth Kramer of Trinity University, San Antonio, Texas. Their help and encouragement were vital to my professional development.

In its first incarnation the present book was a series of monthly lessons for members of the Association for Research and Enlightenment. Cheryl Salerno was very helpful as the editor of this series, and I was much encouraged in the project by the favorable response to these essays by many A.R.E. members. Richard Boyle did the illustrations.

Richard I. Abrams saw the potential for these lessons becoming a book and being given wide distribution. He outlined the book, rewrote the chapters for easier readability, and arranged for its publication with Bantam. I am deeply appreciative of his faith, encouragement, and competent diligence in this project.

Dr. Harold J. Reilly is the source of much of my understanding of the care of the physical body including the "coin word," C.A.R.E., which is the theme of one of the chapters.

The actual writing of the book was made possible and enhanced by the office support of my associates, Dee Shambaugh Sloan and Marilyn Peterson, and by the excellent typing of Ruth Braun.

And I am very appreciative of the gracious response to our manuscript by Bantam Editor, Grace Bechtold.

Herbert Bruce Puryear
Virginia Beach, Virginia
November 24, 1981

CONTENTS

PREFACE

My grandfather, Edgar Cayce, who lived in Virginia Beach, Virginia, conducted a life work which led to his being called America's greatest mystic.

While he was in a sleep-like state, he could see into the future and into the past; he could describe ongoing distant events as they were happening; and he could astound doctors with his vision of the human body. His readings, or spoken words while in this state, were carefully transcribed. Subsequently he has undoubtedly become the most documented psychic who ever lived. The accuracy of his readings and predictions is truly astounding.

The A.R.E., which he founded in 1931 to study and disseminate this information, continues to this day as a membership organization, investigating ways of applying my grandfather's insights.

Having only an eighth-grade education, Edgar Cayce was, by the standards of the world, a plain and simple man. He was as surprised as others by his extraordinary abilities. Deeply religious, he struggled throughout his life to be of aid to those who came to him seeking help. He refused to use his talents for other than helpful purposes. There was a very special quality about this man that attracted and continues to attract people to the story of his life and work, and to the rich and far-reaching information he gave.

Despite the many books written about Edgar Cayce, there has long been a need for an effective and simplified introduction to the philosophy and psychology presented by the readings. In fulfillment of this need, I believe that Dr. Herbert Bruce Puryear has made a major contribution to the literature surrounding the Edgar Cayce phenomena.

Charles Thomas Cayce
President, A.R.E.

8 September 1981
Virginia Beach, Virginia

INTRODUCTION

The purpose of this book is to serve a special function to the seeker. Millions have become familiar with the Edgar Cayce story and have read about his life through one of the biographies such as *There Is A River* by Thomas Sugrue or *Edgar Cayce: The Sleeping Prophet* by Jess Stearn. Stirred by the philosophy of the readings, they don't know what step to take next.

The present book should be of special help to those who would like to take that next step: obtaining an in-depth view of the psychology and philosophy of the readings, presented in a context that will help the reader integrate this information with his own religious background, scientific perspective, and personal life.

Alfred North Whitehead, the great English philosopher and educator, defined philosophy as "the endeavor to formulate a system of general ideas which shall be consistent, coherent and complete, in terms of which every aspect of our experience can be interpreted." We hope the reader will utilize the information in this book, applying Whitehead's standard.

In addition to its philosophical premises, this book contains a *model*, a conceptual picture of the nature of man, which we hope will serve as a framework, facilitating an evaluation of all mankind's experiences: religious, psychical, mystical, pathological, altered states, and everyday consciousness. The purpose of this model is to help us organize and integrate what we already know and to lead us to new and creative insights and further testable hypotheses.

There are several principles frequently reiterated

throughout these chapters. A summary of these may help the reader in a study of this information:

1. The first premise of the Edgar Cayce readings is the *oneness of all force*. This force is Life, Light, and Love. It is God, and God is both Law and Love.

2. We, all of us, are spiritual beings, children of God, with a continuity of life from before the beginning to beyond the end of time. This continuity as it relates to the earth plane introduces concepts of reincarnation, karma, and grace.

3. That which the readings saw as most important in our lives is proper motivation and establishing a criterion for our purposes—what the readings call an ideal. The ideal may serve both to quicken the proper motivation and provide a standard by which to evaluate our decisions.

4. These readings say that we are in a three-dimensional consciousness and we can learn by working with three-dimensional concepts. They speak not only of the triune God, but also the triune nature of man. In every consideration we need to examine the physical, mental and spiritual aspects. The spirit is the life, mind is the builder, and the physical is the result. There is a special stress on the mind as the creative part of ourselves. That upon which we dwell in the mind we become.

5. This information always insists that all questions can be answered if we listen to the Spirit within. We must learn to trust that Spirit for information, guidance, and healing. This is accomplished primarily by practicing the silence in meditation.

6. It is necessary that we put self aside. There is an aspect of us all, the lower self, the primary problem of which is the spirit of rebellion. One day everyone of us must relinquish this self-oriented spirit.

7. This is a philosophy of work, of application, and of service. Edgar Cayce encouraged all to apply what they knew, assuring that when they did, the next step would be given.

A study and application of the principles of these

readings will lead you to a whole new life full of hope and promise for yourself, for your loved ones, and for your relationship to all mankind. As a form of the story of the Gospel, this information, in its truth, richness, depth, beauty, applicability, and accessibility is *good news* indeed.

PART ONE
THE SETTING

Chapter One

SOURCES OF
PSYCHIC INFORMATION

The life of Edgar Cayce is one of the most compelling in the history of mankind. It is a story of self-examination, seeking, and selfless service. For more than forty years, Edgar Cayce conducted a work that has been referred to as giving readings. A reading was a discourse given by Cayce while he was lying down, his eyes closed, in an altered state of consciousness. Almost always delivered in his own normal voice, the discourses were recorded stenographically by Gladys Davis Turner and typed immediately. More than fourteen thousand of these readings are now preserved and available for study. They cover such a wide range of subject matter that they are indexed under more than ten thousand major subject headings. They are to be found in the library of the A.R.E. in Virginia Beach, Virginia.

Most of the readings were given for individuals and, therefore, deal with specific personal questions concerning various aspects of physical, mental, spiritual, vocational, and interpersonal life. Some of these readings, however, were complete discourses on topics such as meditation, Bible interpretation, and world affairs. It was not necessary for the person obtaining the reading to be present: Mr. Cayce was able to describe individuals and diagnose their physical condition with surprising accuracy, even though they might have been hundreds of miles away. Because of these readings, thousands of people were helped, often in ways which transformed their lives. In their entirety, the readings provide specific procedures which are currently helpful in treating many major illnesses. And now, decades after Cayce's death, his readings continue to inspire, educate, and amaze those who research them.

This briefly was Edgar Cayce's work. If we take his psychic readings and their accompanying documentation seriously, they will revolutionize our ordinary notions about our sources of information, or how we come by knowledge.

How Can We Know?

The question, "How can we know?" is one of the most fundamental concerns of all mankind. Every choice we make is influenced by assumptions we have accepted. Every day we make decisions affecting our health, our business affairs, our relationships with our families and others, our mental and our spiritual attitudes.

What are the sources of information upon which we base our decisions? In his search for knowledge, man has turned to many authorities: to a great mind, such as Aristotle's; to divine inspiration, such as the Bible; to personal experience and the physical senses; to reason and to the findings of scientific research.

For thousands of years, and especially since the renaissance, our civilization has been deeply influenced by philosophies which maintain that all knowledge originates in the *outer* world and is mediated by the physical senses. Scientific knowledge is based on this assumption. In contrast, Edgar Cayce, who was really only one exceptional individual among hundreds who have travelled the mystic path, presented solid evidence that information of every kind may be obtained entirely from within.

The Edgar Cayce story raises numerous questions about the inner world as a source of information. How does psychic ability relate to us? What are the pitfalls of turning within? What was the source of the information Edgar Cayce gave? What are the steps we should take in evaluating other sources?

How Does Psychic Ability
Relate to Us?

Let us examine for the moment the word "psychic" which was chosen by the readings to describe this work. Acknowledging that this word could be misconstrued by some, the readings always qualified the definition by stating that "psychic is *of the soul*." Thus the word "psychic" when referred to in the readings, connotes more than just psychic ability. Since we are all "souls," psychic ability as an attribute of the soul, is therefore a potential for everyone.

If we are souls with the capacity for psychic awareness that is not limited by time or space, we can conclude, that by attuning ourselves, as souls, to our inner Source, we will find answers to all of our questions, and solutions to what we call problems.

In the words of the psalmist, ". . . ye are gods; and all of you are children of the Most High." (Ps. 82:6) As children of God, we are spiritual beings. Therefore, when Edgar Cayce speaks of his work as being "psychic" and "of the soul," he is referring to this essential spiritual relationship which *we* have with the divine.

What Are the Difficulties and
Pitfalls of Turning Within?

Even though sensitives such as Edgar Cayce seem to be able to tap a Universal source of knowledge, we may find that we are unable to do the same. When we turn within, we often discover instead that we are faced with an array of voices, feelings, impulses, and experiences.

What is the problem? Experientially, we discover that the very process through which we seek contact with the highest, may also reveal to us the less worthy side of ourselves: envy, greed, possessiveness—aspects of our "lower" self. Discerning the nature of the inner experience has, therefore, been problematic for thousands of years.

Some, who become dismayed by the complexity of this inner world, may oversimplify matters by concluding that information received from within is either from God or the devil. We, as seekers, must be extremely careful to avoid such simplistic evaluations.

What Was the Source that Cayce Tapped?

The Edgar Cayce readings are especially helpful in achieving an understanding of the complexity of the inner life. They clarify matters by dividing the inner world into three basic states of consciousness. Although the levels of consciousness are perhaps innumerable, the readings deal mainly with the conscious, the subconscious, and the superconscious.

This threefold view of the dimensions of consciousness can be illustrated with a cone-shaped diagram.

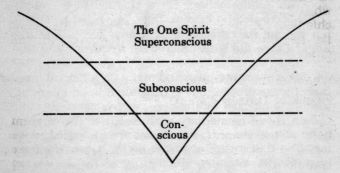

The One Spirit
Superconscious

Subconscious

Conscious

The opening of the cone represents the superconscious, or the access to the Divine, if you will—man's spiritual promise as a soul with unlimited awareness. This level of consciousness, according to the readings, was Edgar Cayce's source of psychic information. The point of the cone represents the physical consciousness which is limited in awareness by the here-and-now requirements of the physical body and its senses. The subconscious, which is evident especially in our dreams and spontaneous urgings, acts as a filter or mediator between the infinite potential of the superconscious and the finite limitations of the waking conscious.

The concept of the subconscious as a dynamic process *between* normal physical consciousness and the superconscious potential is the key to a fuller understanding of the array of inner experiences available to us. As a mediator, the subconscious may either enhance or distort man's access to the divine within. Information coming from the superconscious filters through the thought forms and desire patterns of the subconscious. Therefore, it may be accurate or inaccurate, helpful or harmful, pure or distorted.

Based on the above threefold model, an individual may be said to be psychic to the degree that he is able to put aside the distracting input from the conscious and subconscious in preference to input from the superconscious, which may put him in touch with all worthwhile information. For a channel to be consistently accurate and helpful, then, one must be able to tap the superconscious on a regular basis. And this Edgar Cayce did with remarkable frequency and consistency.

The ability to establish and maintain a helpful input from the superconscious is dependent upon many factors. It is affected by the general physical health and the degree of momentary attunement of the physical body of the channel. It involves the thoughts, emotions, and desires of the channel. It depends on the channel's deep-seated conception of the source he intends to tap. And it is influenced by the purposes, motivations, and ideals of the channel.

Considering such a model of consciousness and the complex role of the subconscious as the mediator between out conscious mind and the Divine, we can begin to understand and properly appreciate the problem of obtaining information from psychic sources.

The Need for Outside Sources

We must also turn outside of ourselves for information. If we have begun to center ourselves by establishing an ideal and by attuning ourselves through meditation, then we can respond constructively to outside sources. Everyone relies to some extent upon externally obtained information.

There is an excellent example in the Old Testament about external sources of information. Shortly before receiving the ten commandments, Moses was visited by his father-in-law, Jethro. Moses recounted to him in full detail all the ways in which God, working through Moses, manifested Himself in the events surrounding the Exodus. The next day Moses sat to judge the people, who had waited from morning till evening. Jethro perceived the inefficiency of this procedure and intimated that Moses should appoint assistants to aid him in judging. Moses gave heed to his father-in-law and did all that he suggested (Exodus 18). Thus Moses, one of the greatest and most direct channels for the word of God, was confident enough to recognize and act upon a good idea from an external source. Like Moses, we need to be open to God working through those around us, since they, too, have access to the Divine within.

The Importance of Having an Ideal

There are many voices from without and from within which clamor for our attention and commitment. Parents, teachers, peers, politicians, advertisers, preachers, psychics, scientists, philosophers, and holy men—all call us to share their point of view.

There are as many voices from within as without: pride, jealousy, fear, self-esteem, biological urges, concern for what others might think, dreams, discarnate entities of every ilk, guardian angels, a dozen forms of conscience both healthy and pathological, and the still small voice.

With all this input, how can we fail to be as corks tossed by every wave and ripple? We need a solid place to stand, a place to which we may return, when we need to reevaluate and reorient our lives and thoughts. We need a firm and stable criterion by which to measure information. Unless we assume the initiative and responsibility for establishing such a criterion in our own lives, we should not expect ourselves to be other than wavering and often misled.

For this reason, among others, Edgar Cayce said that the most important experience for any person was to establish a spiritual ideal. The concept of setting the ideal is challenging and beautiful. It is establishing a motivational center of gravity, a hub, or a core within. As we become centered, we have a stable platform from which to gain the optimum point of view on every question. Setting the ideal is establishing a quality of spirit that is related to motivation, desire, purpose, intention, and incentive. It provides a measuring rod by which to make comparisons, but it is also an internal centering which automatically gives us a clearer perception of every issue.

The use of the ideal as a standard constitutes a mature step forward over measuring new information on the basis of previous experience, training, or beliefs.

How do we establish an ideal? Simply by writing it down on a piece of paper. It may be a name such as Moses or Jesus or Buddha which awakens within us a high sense of purpose; it may be a phrase or an affirmation; or it may be a word for a quality such as *love* or *oneness*. If we review the ideal, allowing it to quicken within us the high spirit which it connotes, and if we measure choices and decisions by this spirit, it will in time transform our lives as well as give us a stable point of view by which to evaluate sources of information. The readings say, "The key should be making, compelling, inducing, having the mind one with that which is the ideal." (262–84)

Evaluating the Work of a Psychic

Those who've heard of Edgar Cayce may naturally ask if anyone today is giving readings using Edgar Cayce's method. Yes, there are many; but the crucial question is how we evaluate their work. This question should be considered from several perspectives.

First, Edgar Cayce's foremost desire in seeking information for another person was that he would try to obtain only that which would be helpful and hopeful. The motive behind eliciting psychic information—whether it is sought within ourselves or through another channel—is of utmost importance. So, in considering the work of a psychic or outer source, we might ask ourselves, "Is this work helpful and hopeful?"

Second, another characteristic quality of Edgar Cayce's information is its urging everyone to seek attunement with the Divine within himself. The readings' emphasis upon personal attunement and practical application helps us personally to accept responsibility for growth rather than expecting it to be handed to us.

So a second question that we need to ask in evaluating a psychic source is, "To what degree does this information agree with my own intuition and stimulate me to *actively apply* what I know?"

Third, the history of all living faiths is punctuated from their origins to the present-day with leaders, healers, and teachers who have been sources of guidance, information, and inspiration to those whom they served. Some have worked within organizational structures, others have worked outside of them, and some have served in both ways. The work of the Spirit on behalf of the souls of men has been carried forward by such dedicated individuals. Thus, a third question which may aid us in evaluating psychic sources is, "Does this work build upon the best contributions of previously helpful sources?"

Finally, we need to ask ourselves, "Does this psychic

information interfere with my devotion to the highest reality?"

From these four perspectives we come to understand that having an external source of direction or healing may ultimately work for or against our seeking and developing attunement to the Spirit within. Thus, we may also recognize both the legitimate work of psychics *and* why it is often not in our best interests to depend upon external sources of guidance if we are to grow in our own inner attunement.

There are, to be sure, teachers and psychic sources who may help us clarify the direction of our lives. But the crucial question is, "Where do I place my trust?" In others? In myself? Or in the Divine within? If it is the Divine, then seeking through outside sources should take place only in response to guidance from within— not as a substitute for it.

Summary

If we set our own ideal and are focused in our purposes; if we turn within in the silence, maintaining a spirit of, "Be Thou the guide"; and if we place our trust fully in the Divine, we will be given the next step. The information we need may be offered to us directly as it was to Moses. Or the information may come through another source, such as the Bible, a physician, a counselor, a minister, a teacher, or a psychic.

Chapter Two

ATTUNEMENT AND APPLICATION

We wonder most about ourselves. Why are we so imprisoned in the here and now, in a universe so unimaginably immense? We wonder about our relationship to the people around us—near and far, small and great. We wonder, Why? Why am I the way I am? Why are they the way they are? Why am I failing? Why am I succeeding? Why am I ill? Why am I well when others are ill? Why is this relationship going the way it is? Why can't I know what to do? Why can't I be free to be what I want to be? Why is there so much suffering? Why can't I be happy?

We look about for answers. We look to that family member, neighbor, or friend who seems to have something special that we do not have. We look to the famous for a vicarious glimpse of the good life, and we look to the great for meaning. We find that we learn all too slowly and reluctantly and painfully.

We must first become *the seeker*! When we become seekers, we not only put into action the following universal law but we also claim it as a promise—Seek, and you shall find.

Becoming the Seeker

There is much to learn! We are quick to acknowledge that we do not know all there is to know about chemistry or physics or such. We anticipate new developments in every field of human endeavor except those that deal with "religion." We say that we "believe in" or "don't believe in" certain teachings. Many of these issues are not just matters of belief but matters of fact, which rest upon truths about the nature of man and the universe. Either the universe works in certain lawful ways or it does not; we should anticipate progress in understanding these universal laws. Perhaps the major problem has been in failing to differentiate between knowing *what* we believe and knowing *in whom* we believe.

How ready are we to grow in a deeper understanding? Growth may mean change and change may be painful! As we become seekers, where are we to turn?

We know that we gain most in insight and inspiration from history's great teachers; yet, we resist accepting their gifts. We resist the light they would share with us because of imagined differences of background, culture, language, tradition, and beliefs. We may search out some flaw or generate some misgiving to avoid an encounter with the greater wisdom these teachers might share with us. Because we are fearful and unsure of ourselves, we cling to beliefs which, even in our own minds, are inadequate and sometimes untenable.

If we could just get a real and living sense that Moses does not belong only to the Jews, nor does Jesus belong only to the Christians, Gautama does not belong only to the Buddhists, Mohammed does not belong only to Islam, Mahatma Gandhi does not belong only to India, George Washington Carver does not belong only to the blacks, and Helen Keller does not belong only to the handicapped!

With a more open attitude toward our fellowman, we could lay claim to a much broader and enriching world view. Instead we permit narrow-mindedness and dogmatism, unfortunate childhood experiences, or imagined limitations of background and tradition to rob us of the riches to be gleaned from the lives of these great people—gifts that are for all to claim. The more we treasure a sense of the value of humanity, the more surely we must sense that we share it with all others. The simple decency of acknowledging the essential interrelatedness of all life in the world should be accompanied by a more profound awareness of the brotherhood of all.

Now our seeking has led us to consider the life and work of Edgar Cayce. He is just such an example of insight and inspiration for all who will accept the gifts presented through him. Yet his readings which were documented, tested, and verified, and through which thousands have been helped and healed, were also represented by him as containing nothing new. This should not come as a surprise, because the central truth to which this information would lead us is what all spiritual teachers have affirmed; and the essence of this truth, which is always twofold, may be found in these words: Attunement and Application. All that we truly long for lies within the depths of our own innermost being; but to become our own it must be lived in our actions.

Thus, these two words together constitute an action form of the great commandment: "To love God with all our heart, mind, and soul" is *attunement*. "To love our neighbor as ourselves" is *application*.

Attunement

Can we deny that everything we value most deeply is a product of the human mind? All of the sciences, inventions, the arts, the creative manifestations, the sacred literatures have developed because of individual minds struggling for a kind of perfection. Yet creative people have often sensed that they were simply channels through which a greater reality was being expressed. Attunement is a quickening, an elevation of consciousness. It puts us in touch with that *greater reality*. We know this to be so, yet perhaps we have thought that deep attunement was possible only for the great, or reserved for others, but surely not something we could do anything about or practice on our own. Yet each of us may discover that only by seeking and growing in inner attunement, does each of us come to know our own unique and individual WAY.

Attunement to what? What is the essence of our inner being? What is that *greater reality* which has been the source of creative inspiration of the great contributors to mankind's heritage? Many have difficulty in referring to this *reality* as God. Some prefer the term "Creative Forces." The Edgar Cayce readings work with a first premise of Oneness, the Oneness of all force—the Law of One. Regarding attunement, the readings speak in the strongest terms of a personal quality of this *reality*, a reality which each of us can experience.

Application

In most areas of life, it is all too apparent that diligent, energetic, persistent application is regularly accompanied by uncommon success. This relationship between application and accomplishment is so obvious that were we not aware of a few seeming exceptions, we would call it a universal law. However, even though we see this principle working in certain obvious ways, as in productivity in a factory, we may not see how it may work in healing our bodies or developing healthy family relationships. In *all* areas of life, when we apply what we know, we come out ahead.

Nothing hinders us more than saying one thing and doing another. Yet all of us *know* more of what constitutes a "better way" in many aspects of our life than we are willing to apply. There is a quality within us which deters us from doing our best. If we could identify and confront that quality, accept responsibility for it and not project it upon others, we would take a great step toward our own better well-being.

All that is asked of any of us as souls is that we do what we presently know to do. When we do what we know to do, the next step is already given. There is a saying from the East that when the student is ready, the teacher will appear. This often is taken to mean that a person will appear as a master; however, another way of understanding this truth is that when we bring ourselves to the point of being truly ready to learn, the learning experience needed will be forthcoming. We may think of ourselves as being ready to learn only insofar as we are applying what we already know.

Motivation and the Ideal

All of us have often said to ourselves, "If only I could bring myself to do what I know I am capable of doing. If only I could get motivated." We recognize a vital ingredient that some people seem to have and others do not. Or we find that this quality seems to come automatically in some areas of our lives and not at all in others. Motivation seems to comprise a major dimension of what really counts in life.

There is a whole cluster of concepts which are related

to this dimension of motivation: intention, incentive, desire, purpose, aspiration, the spirit in which we act, the ideal. We recognize the *intensity* of motivation when we say someone is highly or poorly motivated. We also recognize its *quality* when we speak of being selfless or self-centered in our motivation.

The Cayce readings emphasize the crucial nature of this dimension of life when they stress that ". . . the most important experience of this or any individual entity is to first know what *is* the ideal—spiritually." (357–13) By the word "ideal," the readings refer to the standard of quality of motivation by which we measure our decisions and actions.

Here is a difference! Rather than taking our motivation for granted as an unknown and unchangeable given (i.e., "That's just the way I am."), we are told to *set* an *ideal* by an act of our own will, to choose a *standard* of motivation by which we as individuals intend to measure our decisions and with which we wish to quicken our actions.

Thus, the first step in becoming motivated is to choose as a standard the quality of motivation which we want to have as the driving force behind our actions.

The second step is to dwell upon this quality with the mind—not the intellect—but the imaginative forces of the mind. The key consists in inducing the mind to dwell upon the ideal. As we require the imaginative forces of the mind to dwell upon a high ideal, we are actually selecting the motivational circuitry in the body through which the life force may flow.

An ideal is not something we make happen or attain; it is something we allow to flow through us. If we set "love" as an ideal, still we cannot *of ourselves* love. However, by establishing love as a standard or ideal, by dwelling upon love in the mind, and by acting in accord with love as a standard for behavior, we begin to permit the power of love to *flow through* us. As the spirit of love flows through us it begins to transform our lives and the lives of those about us.

The Purpose of the Work of Edgar Cayce

Edgar Cayce often commented on the purpose of his work. The essence of what he said is contained in a statement given as a motto for the work: "To make manifest the love of God and man." (254-42) This again is an application of the great commandment: to love God with all of our heart, mind, and soul; and to love our neighbor as ourselves. The motto means, essentially, to *live* the great commandment.

On one occasion, Edgar Cayce was asked to comment on the "correct attitude . . . in order to maintain and keep first and foremost before self and the public the correct ideals of the Association for Research and Enlightenment (A.R.E.)." To this he replied:

". . . the simplicity of the ability of individuals to apply that as may be obtained from their own subconscious self, cosmic forces and universal consciousness (or call it by whatever name the individual may choose)—this is the great truth that must be apparent to the layman, the individual, the scientist, the mathematician, the historian, the individual seeking information through these sources finds this apparent . . . that this force is apparent in the earth's development at this time through another form or manner is only an expression to individuals that all are a portion of the divine, the creative energy, the whole, and this purpose kept first and foremost is that sure success of the approach of committee, individual, and Association, to the public."

254-46

Notice how attunement and application appear in this reading: the simplicity of the ability of individuals to *apply* that as may be obtained from their own inner *attunement*.

Now, consider the second half of the reading which refers to Edgar Cayce himself: ". . . that this force (Edgar Cayce as its vehicle) is apparent in the earth's development . . . through another form . . . is only the expression . . . that all are a portion of the divine." In other words, the extraordinary work of Edgar Cayce, including his ability to tune in to the cosmic forces and universal consciousness was a demonstration of the simplicity of the principle that all of us are a portion of and can attune to the divine, not by using a phrase as a catchword, but rather by living the exemplary life.

Experiencing the helpfulness of the readings does not at all require that we "believe" in them, but rather that we regard the information as worthy of examination and potentially helpful. Instead of endorsing the readings as a direct source of guidance, we should think of them primarily as a source of encouragement and instruction on how to attune to the Spirit within. The specific information in the readings is to be *tried*, not *believed in*. Try it. If it helps, fine; if not, leave it alone.

Summary and Some Next Steps

Our challenge always entails two dimensions: the right spirit or attunement, and the right application. The right spirit is begun by establishing an ideal and by dwelling upon that ideal in daily meditation. Right application grows out of choosing to act upon our best attunement and understanding.

You can begin now with the following next steps:

First, take a piece of paper, a journal or diary or a dream recording book. Write a list of words which have an impact upon you, elicit a sense of high or proper motivation. Choose one word and begin to dwell upon it, making decisions based upon the quality of motivation which is awakened by that word.

Next, begin to establish a daily quiet time upon which to base a later practice of regular meditation. Set a specific daily time period. During this period, read something of your choice which quickens within you a high sense of meaning and purpose. Read and reread this again and again.

Then, choose one thing in your life which you have been intending to change for the better. Write it down. Bring this resolution repeatedly into relationship with the word you have chosen as an ideal. Seek in your quiet time to be given the needed energy and proper attitude to bring about this change in your life.

Chapter Three

REINCARNATION

The great manifestations of the universe are life and consciousness. The great mysteries of the universe are the continuity of life and our ever expanding consciousness of God. Beyond the manifestations of life are intimations at every turn of its continuity. A seed falls into the ground, dies, only to return again in a resurrection to a new life. The seasons return again and again manifesting birth, growth, fruition and death, then birth again in continuity of life. For man, the experience of life is inseparable from the experience of consciousness. But, beyond the immediate personal experience of consciousness, we have a greater sense of awakening, enrichment, and expansion. We are continually growing in our awareness of our relationship with others, the universe about us, and the Divine.

Our understanding of the continuity of life of the individual soul and of its growing awareness of its Oneness with God is greatly expanded and enhanced by the concept of reincarnation. As a concept, reincarnation is very complex, involving many principles. For one who has begun to consider it for the first time, the connotations of the word "reincarnation" may have little relationship to the true meaning of this great insight into the nature of man.

The Pilgrimage of the Soul

The approach of the Edgar Cayce readings to reincarnation has beauty, sensitivity, depth, complexity, and applicability not exceeded in any other body of information. In order to understand this approach, we must consider the greater story of the journey of the soul.

We were all created in the beginning as spiritual beings, children of God, born of His desire for companionship, with the potential to become cocreators with Him. As souls, we were given minds with which to build, wills with which to choose, and access to the Spirit, the one great force of the universe. We were perfect from the day of our creation. Then, born of our own pride, a rebellious turn of spirit occurred within us and we went astray. We made a succession of choices which were not in harmony with universal laws; we built limiting thought patterns with our minds; and by these we enveloped and encased ourselves in lower and lower dimensions of consciousness.

In our movement through the universe as a wave of souls, we came upon the three-dimensional manifestations of the earth plane. We saw, were attracted to, and projected our consciousness into an ongoing evolutionary development of life. As one manifestation of the spirit of God, the earth was good and beautiful; but we were not intended to invest our consciousness in it to such an extent that we would forfeit our freedom, forget our royal heritage, and lose our ability to move through other dimensions of the universe.

Our *entrapment* in the earth was not at all due to the evil nature of the flesh but rather to the limiting effect of our own thought forms and desire patterns. Imagine a swimmer who ties a rock around his waist so that he may walk on the ocean floor. He struggles to the surface for a breath but is drawn down again by the weight. There is nothing evil about experiencing the ocean floor but the rock about his waist draws him away from his true source of life. He is no longer free. The rocks about our waists are our own thought forms and desire patterns. Even after death, they may focus our consciousness away from an awareness of our oneness with God and draw us back again into the earth experience. Thus entrapped, it is as though our souls are dead; yet, God calls to us again and again, Choose life!

The Plan for Life

Out of His love for His children, God converted the earth from an evolving garden of paradise into a school (or hospital) for the souls of man. A plan was established to enable us, as souls, to become free from the entrapment which we had built for ourselves. Quickly, even as man measures time, the pattern for the human body was manifested. It was to be a temple in which the soul could come to an awareness of its Oneness with the Father. It was prepared specifically, both as an instrument for attunement and as a system for continuing survival and social development in the earth plane. With the coming of man, from Adam to Noah, the forces of the universe set limitations so that souls could incarnate only in a human form. We were to be permitted no longer to intervene directly in the ongoing evolution of the earth by projecting into thought forms or other life forms. With the development of an appropriate vehicle for growth and attunement, we, as souls, were given a new and special opportunity to begin the long journey home through successive incarnations.

The *pattern* portion of this plan for the redemption of souls was completed with the life, death, and resurrection of Jesus. The pattern which was begun with Adam was not fully manifested—a pattern made in the image of God and lived out in a life fully attuned and obedient to the will of God. Through this pattern and by means of His power, there was now a very special *way* prepared for the souls' return to an awareness of their oneness with God. It was a pattern of obedience to the Spirit, crucifixion of the lower self, and loving service.

How Does Reincarnation Work?

The soul entering into the body may be likened to a person entering a car. After driving the car for some time, it becomes irreparable and is discarded. Later, the owner, maintaining the same preference, obtains another similar car. His choices at this point are limited by his own tastes and resources. The analogy is instructive for helping us understand certain processes; however, it is not adequate to convey a full understanding of the incarnation process. We have three bodies: spiritual, mental, and physical. When we incarnate, the spiritual body and the mental body are projected into and manifested through the physical body. Thus, the physical manifestation is more fully a projection of the fabric of our very being than is implied in the analogy of simply selecting an automobile on the basis of previous preferences.

The Law of Karma

The saying that "like begets like" provides an integral insight into the laws of the universe. This principle works at the heart of the dynamics of reincarnation. Every manifestation of life reproduces *each after its own kind.* The same is true with the thoughts, choices, and behavior of man. A central teaching of the New Testament still relatively unexamined in its implications is: "Whatsoever a man sows, that shall he also reap." (Galatians 6:7)

In the Sanskrit, this principle has been termed Karma, meaning *action* or the law of continuity of action, "like begetting like."

This beautiful law establishes order and cosmos instead of disorder and chaos in the universe. This lawfulness issues from the very nature and love of God. Mankind depends upon it in every manifestation of the universe about him. But we are dismayed by this law-fulness when we experience it in meeting the consequences of our own self-oriented thoughts, choices, and actions. Although we may experience it in pain, this law reveals an aspect of the nature of God as a manifestation of the consistency and persistency of His love. In its working, it has the effect of awakening, turning, quickening, and reminding us that we cannot be gods apart from God, that we are part of the whole, that we must align ourselves with universal law, and that we are responsible for our relationships with other souls. The soul's return in successive incarnations is not God's requirement for payment or punishment. It is rather out of His love that we are permitted again and again another opportunity to choose the way of life, light, and love.

Comparing the effects of choices and actions on our being with the effects of foods being assimilated in the body is an analogy used in the readings for discussing how karma works. The previous life experiences are not just archival records of the distant past. They imbue the very substance of our present lives. They manifest in the cell structure of our bodies, our facial features, our predispositions toward certain diseases such as alcoholism or allergies, our emotions, talents, appetites, and in our reactions toward others and the universe about us.

With the death of the physical body, the mental and spiritual bodies remain much the same with respect to patterns and purposes. We move to the experiences and planes of consciousness that we have prepared for ourselves. We process our earth experiences at the mental level, review the lessons learned, and begin to prepare for a proper time and occasion to return in which we resume our lessons and our pilgrimage toward oneness with God, with the universe, and with our fellow man. By the law, "like attracts like," we are drawn to parents, bodies, circumstances, and relationships with others, all of which are specifically appropriate for each soul.

How Does Reincarnation Relate
to Our Religion?

Sometimes we have an expectation that if anything is true or important, it would necessarily have been presented to us earlier in our learning experiences or religious traditions. However, let us consider what we presently know about electricity and compare that with what was known only two hundred years ago—which was almost nothing. Electricity, the building block of the universe, a secret of the ages until only recently, has appeared in the consciousness of man today in such a way that there is hardly any experience in our lives that is not affected by man's utilization of it.

Just as we may not find the word "electricity" in the Bible, we may not find the word "reincarnation." What we do find, however, are some principles and laws whose richness and beauty can be fully appreciated only with an understanding of the continuity of life and the cycle of return.

In the New Testament, one of the very direct references to reincarnation in the teachings of Jesus is His affirmation of the identity of John the Baptist as the prophet Elijah, who was to return. (Matthew 11:14 and Malachi 4:5) For many, such passages are not convincing. The resistance of some religious teachers to the concept of reincarnation is related more to problems of emotion and motivation than to problems of reason and scripture. The readings indicate that the reason reincarnation has not been retained in Christianity has been a desire to take shortcuts. Many hope that by belonging to a certain organization, sect or belief system, or by claiming a certain affirmation of faith that they will in some special way find favor with God and thus be ushered directly into His presence upon their deaths.

The teaching that there is only one life and after that eternal judgment, is based in part on a kind of elitism. Each individual, group, denomination or country that believes it has discovered the true way, feels superior to others who do not hold to their own insights.

In turn, the teaching that there is only one life lends itself to exploitation. If one person, group, or church by whatever name, has access to *the* way and others do not, then extraordinary control may be wielded over individuals, groups, and nations. The threat of excommunication is an extreme example. Social pressure is subtler but very powerful. Many souls have been diverted from a search for *truth* by their peers implying their interests were not quite respectable. The concept of reincarnation may be resisted because it nullifies all sense of individual superiority, which one may hold simply by virtue of belonging to a certain group, race, sex, belief system or nation. We are taught in the Bible that God is the Father of all and He is no respecter of persons. Reincarnation is the great leveler of all mankind.

There are many misunderstandings of the religious implications of reincarnation. But whatever our understanding of the plan of redemption, it should be enriched by the concept of reincarnation. It is only in terms of reincarnation that we can think of God as being truly fair, patient, loving, forgiving, and all-merciful. His commitment as a Good Shepherd is to bring *all* His lost sheep into the fold. He is the Father of all souls; it is not His will that any soul should perish; and if God be for us, who can be against us?

How Does Reincarnation Affect Our Daily Lives?

The relevance of reincarnation to our daily lives is not so much in understanding *who* we were in terms of name, date, and place but rather *what* we were, so that we may understand why things are the way they are at this very moment in our lives. All of us have wondered about the uniqueness of the individual experience—why we were born into the circumstances that we were; why we encountered specific individuals and situations in our childhood; why we seem to have certain talents and abilities in some areas and are lacking those in others; why we are drawn strongly to some people and repelled by others. As we come to understand that things are the way they are for a reason, we can begin to see the lawfulness behind each of these circumstances.

The concept of reincarnation enables us to understand how, in meeting various situations, we are meeting ourselves. As we assume responsibility for placing ourselves in a particular circumstance, we may avoid the otherwise almost inevitable paranoid quality of thinking which continually blames others for our problems. As we grow in understanding that each encounter is meeting of self, we may also grow in a willingness to assume responsibility for our choices, as well as their consequences.

Most importantly, we must learn that in our present state of consciousness, we cannot save ourselves. Although there is a law that we reap what we sow, it also means that if we sow forgiveness, we reap forgiveness a hundredfold. As we forgive ourselves and others, we are forgiven. There is no life or growth in attunement except by the love and grace of God.

Although the law of karma helps us to understand why we are the way we are and to accept responsibility for ourselves, we must not live our lives by attitudes based on this law. Rather, as we attune within, we should live in an awareness of the living spirit of God, Who in His love is eager to heal and transform us and to change our stumbling blocks into stepping-stones.

How to Know What You Were

The readings affirm that it is as important to know whence we came as it is to know whither we are going. Yet many ask: "If reincarnation is so important, why do I have no memory of these previous experiences?"

Our bodies, as the present vehicles of the soul, contain within them all records of the soul from the beginning. By the grace of God and in the dimension of time, we meet ourselves step by step. Our problems, our lessons to be learned, and our great talents are unfolded in dosages that we can manage and assimilate. These heritages of the soul lie dormant within us, awaiting the necessary progress on the path and the proper quickening by the Spirit. In due season, we may begin to remember who we are and the nature of our royal heritage.

As we seek a deeper personal knowledge of the details of previous lives, we should seek in terms of what really matters in our present lives. It is not so much the precise names, places, and times as it is the quality of the life. How deep goes our relationship with others? What is the nature of present responsibilities? What strengths and weaknesses of character are we presently manifesting? What are our hopes and fears? Only after probing may we find in the concept of reincarnation a basis for understanding such questions.

The regular recording of dreams has been a rich source of previous life information for many who have pursued this approach. Some who received life readings from Edgar Cayce subsequently had dreams which provided insights related to previous lives, as convincing and applicable as the readings themselves.

To get some ideas about previous life circumstances, begin an inventory of what you know about yourself. What were some of your childhood longings? What historical periods interest you? What foreign countries have you visited or would you most like to visit? What are your attitudes toward various nationalities? What are the interests and talents which are natural to you? What are your present religious interests and biases? What music and paintings intrigue you? What are your favorite foods? As you answer these questions, you will discover that you know more about your previous lives than you imagined.

We may begin to rediscover our true selves and to

remember who we are and where we are going, as we set ourselves on the path, establish our ideals, and begin to practice meditation, attuning the body and mind to the Spirit within.

Chapter Four

CITIZENS OF THE UNIVERSE

Scarcely more than five hundred years ago, nearly everyone in the world believed the earth to be flat. Now it is a commonplace belief not only that the earth is round, but that we are also in a solar system, a galaxy, a universe of unimaginable magnitude. If we have progressed so much in our understanding of the psychial universe, could we not similarly progress in our understanding of the nature of man? Can we not remove a layer of limitation from our consciousness, another layer, and yet another? And can we then entertain the *full* implications that derive from understanding that the nature of man is *spiritual*?

For thousands of years the religions of the world have revealed to us that there is more to man than his physical being and that there is a greater reality beyond what we experience in physical consciousness. For the past hundred years or more, the field of psychical research has amassed an overwhelming array of experiential data, objective observations, and scientific experiments that have demonstrated in a very substantial manner that there is more to the nature of man and more to reality than we have permitted ourselves to imagine.

Beingness Through Time

One of the dimensions of our "beingness" which we need to reexamine is the continuity of the existence of individuality. Let us consider the possibilities.

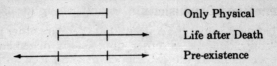

In the diagram above we may designate the biological view of man as "only physical" by a single, short line. Existence begins at birth and ends at death. A next possibility, indicated by the second line, is that existence begins at birth, but continues beyond physical death. This possibility immediately raises considerations of the locus of the consciousness of the individual beyond physical death. It implies another plane of reality. If individuality of consciousness can continue without the physical body, then we are immediately confronted with the question of why we think it begins with physical birth? And so, a third consideration would be that the line which represents continuing individuality extends, not only forward indefinitely, but backward indefinitely. Thus we have the concept of preexistence.

If there is a continuity of individuality beyond physical death, then there must be an existence or "beingness" in a plane or dimension other than the physical, as we presently understand it. Occasionally some people discover themselves in a "new" or another consciousness which may be so commanding that they become convinced it is the only other reality existing. But if we permit any consideration of a life beyond death of the physical body, then we are directly confronted with the possibility of many planes and dimensions of existence.

The Edgar Cayce readings offer us a view of man's nature which, when accepted, will revolutionize our present attitudes about ourselves and others. The magnitude of this revolution will far exceed the movement in consciousness from flat-earth to round-earth awareness. These readings give a view of man as a spiritual being, revealing that we are not only citizens of the universe as we know it (the physical universe) but also of other, many other, planes of consciousness.

Planes and Dimensions

Let us consider the concept that there are other planes of consciousness or other dimensions of experience. We understand the experience in the earth as three-dimensional. We hear of a fourth dimension. (At this point, we're not even considering the nature of a fifth, a sixth, or a seventh dimension.)

For example, let us imagine a building with several floors, each of which has several rooms. Now we may consider going from one room to another on the same level, or moving from one level upward or downward to other levels. As we try to understand the kinds of experiences that people of different orientations have—whether psychic, mystical, or religious—we may by analogy consider whether they've moved into another room or another level. It is probable that some who can move from one level to another do not necessarily have the ability to go into all rooms or to move through all levels. To illustrate, a trance medium has a spirit guide whose focal point of consciousness resides in another plane. This is like an elevator which may move from the first floor to the third. As many buildings have elevators that are limited in movement to only one specific floor, so it is probable that many who can move in consciousness out of the limitations of this plane may move consistently only to one other level. Because the reality at this other level may be so convincing, so accurate, and so consistent, the one experiencing such an awareness may come to think that that is all there is on "the other side." And so, we have discrepancies between perceptions of different psychics or limitations of different mystics' experiences, which may be dogmatized into various belief systems.

Now let us further illustrate these considerations with some specific examples. A number of years ago, a group of us in London were visited by several psychics. One, whose special ability was to read the human aura, described what she saw in the auric field of an individual from our group. Later, another psychic visited us and read the auric field of the same individual. While it was quite clear that the second psychic had seen every aspect of the individual sensed by the first psychic, he'd also experienced dimensions or awarenesses that went far beyond the perceptions of the first.

A second example: We observed a medium who seemed to be able to attune to the spirit plane and to contact and give messages from a deceased individual. Here we have an example of a person moving from the "first floor" to the "third floor" in levels of awareness. However, she reported on a second deceased individual whom she could not contact directly, but who could relay messages through the first individual. The first seemed to be able, in his state beyond the physical, to attune to a plane beyond his own in which the second individual was working. Thus, we might say that the first individual seemed to reside on level three and was able to relay to the medium on level one a message from another individual residing at level four or beyond.

Here is another type of experience. A man who is well known for his ability to travel in consciousness outside the physical body (astral projection) was speaking of how he leaves his grosser body and works in a subtler body. When asked if he had ever been able to leave that subtler body and move to another dimension of an even more subtler experience, he replied that he had indeed been able to do that on one occasion.

Beyond the limited experiences and perceptions reported, the information given in the Cayce readings reveals that the extent of our citizenship in the universe is virtually unlimited! As spiritual beings, we not only existed before our entry into the earth plane, but we were, in previous times, able to move through many dimensions and planes. Although our present assignment seems to be in the earth in a three-dimensional consciousness, the cycle of the soul's experience, even here, relates more to *the entire solar system*, not just in the earth plane. This solar system experience has within it eight planes of consciousness, of which the earth represents the third. Other dimensions of consciousness are associated with other planets. Cayce did not give a complete and systematic description of these; however, the following incomplete chart was derived from two readings as an illustration.

DIMENSION	PLANET	ATTRIBUTE
2	Mercury	pertaining of Mind
	Mars	of Madness (Wrath?)
3	Earth	as of Flesh
4	Venus	as Love
7	Jupiter	as Strength
1	Saturn	as of the beginning of earthly woes . . .
8	Uranus	as of Psychic
	Neptune	as of Mystic
	Septimus	as of Consciousness
	Arcturus	as of the developing

CAYCE READINGS: 5002–1; 900–10

There is not only incarnation and reincarnation in the earth plane, but experiences in other planes between incarnations. These experiences are related to the dimension symbolized by the planet. Just as our experiences in the earth plane follow from karmic patterns of our own making in previous lives, so these planetary sojourns are lawfully engaged by that which we have built with our minds. The previous life experiences in the earth are primarily responsible for the karmic patterns of an *emotional* nature. The previous life experiences in other planes are responsible for patterns of a more *mental* or *innate* nature.

Other Dimensions

What are the other dimensions like? Someone once asked Cayce to describe the seventh dimension. He replied that the person didn't even understand the three dimensions he was in, so how could he understand seven? Another asked Cayce to describe the experiences of sojourns in Jupiter, to which he replied that this could be done if the individual understood Jupiterian!

Even so, there were intimations, at least, of how we might understand the fourth dimension. The readings indicate that the best definition of the fourth dimension is an *idea*. Where does it begin? Where does it end? Where can it project? It is without limitation. As an illustration, Cayce asked someone to consider a book. What is real about the book? Its physical dimensions? Its color? Its binding? Or the content, the ideas contained therein? Quickly we can see how, if we have read a good and important book, that the reality of that experience for us was most truly the *ideas* in the book.

Since the fourth dimension relates to the realm of ideas and since the mind is the builder, we may think of this as a level at which patterns are developed; and all we see about us is the energy of the One Force projected through fourth-dimensional patterns into third-dimensional manifestation. We may thus understand how precognition and prophecy are possible as we consider that the sensitive, viewing these, may be reading the fourth-dimensional blueprint prior to its projection into third-dimensional manifestation. This illustration also enables us to understand how prophecy may be changed. The blueprint may be altered by our choices, and the patterns viewed at one time may thus be modified before they are manifested in the earth plane.

Earth Plane Consciousness

Now let us consider our present consciousness. Because we are in a third-dimensional plane, we experience reality as triune and understand all aspects of the One reality better by utilizing triune concepts. Thus we speak of man as physical, mental, and spiritual. We understand the dimensions of man's awareness to be conscious, subconscious, and superconscious. We characterize the world about us as mineral, plant, and animal. We conceptualize the Divine as Father, Son, and Holy Spirit. And we experience the One Force in the dimensions of space, time, and patience.

We speak of space as three-dimensional: height, length, and width; and time as three-dimensional: past, present and future; although in time and space we see that each is a dimension in itself. In the Cayce readings the third of the three dimensions is referred to as *patience*. To understand why Cayce used this word, we need to redefine patience and also to understand patience in its deeper implications. First, let us say that patience is an active force. As a force it is of the One Force, and thus is of the Spirit. It relates to qualities that we value highly in ourselves and others, the qualities of motivation, purpose, intention, and ideals. And it relates to understanding that *things are the way they are for a reason.* Excercising patience means bringing the Spirit to bear on the present circumstances whatever they may be.

To illustrate these dimensions, let us imagine ourselves looking out a window observing a construction crew building a highway. Day after day we see the work carried on. This is *time.* Successive steps lead to the manifested completion of the road. This expression in manifestation represents *space.* Neither of these apparent manifestations of reality is as important as the third consideration: Why are they building a road in this place at this time? When we consider that the most important aspect of this activity is the motivation or purpose, then we get a sense of the reality of *patience* as a dimension.

Other Neighbors

We are just beginning to sense that everyone in the earth is our neighbor—four billion souls. If there exist many other planes of consciousness, are there other souls not presently incarnate in the earth? Another four billion, perhaps, or forty or four hundred billion?

Are we the only kind of beings God could think of? In a physical universe in which the sun is hardly a speck of dust, are we the only children of an Infinite God? Does not our own Bible speak of other orders of beings—angels, archangels, cherubim, and seraphim?

We hear of guardian angels and may wonder about our own. In the New Testament Jesus warns us about the guardian angels of others: "Take heed that ye despise not one of these little ones; for I say unto you, That in heaven their angels do always behold the face of my Father which is in heaven." (Matthew 18:10) If we study Greek mythology, ascertaining how certain gods favored certain mortals and pled their cases before Zeus, the god of gods, and if we consider that each of us has guardian angels beholding the face of the Father, we may be instructed in some measure of the urgency of putting things right with our fellowman.

Some are convinced that at higher levels of consciousness there will not be the limitations of personhood and individual relationships. Do we not measure the stature of a person by the depth of his concern for others? And would that not count even more at a higher level of awareness?

Some are still struggling with the concept of God. Others feel they have grown beyond such limited concepts. Much of their kind of thought, it seems, is based on the attitude: "If I can't think it, then it can't be!" One sometimes wonders if ants believe in man! If we cannot think God with our finite minds, the higher consciousness, such as that tapped through the Cayce readings, may mediate for us. And this amazing source of information affirms His being. Thus, the readings give us a concept of God that is *personal*, yet one not limited by our own finite notions of *person*.

And what about Satan? Some philosophies teach that there are two forces—one for good and one for evil. The great Judeo-Christian insight of Oneness affirms that there is One Force and that He permits His children to make choices which, when out of harmony, give reality to evil. Thus, within the body and beingness of God, of Good, there are points of evil wherever there is the rebellious spirit.

In Job 1:6 we are told that the sons of God came together and Satan also came among them. We may think of Lucifer as a powerful fallen archangel, but in that *one* passage in the Bible which mentions him, he is described as a *man.* (Isaiah 14:16)

If we could take the simple but tremendously dramatic lesson of the unthinkable magnitude of the physical universe and apply it to our need for an expanded awareness of the meaning of being, it would open to us a universe of universes. And we would find ourselves invited to be full-fledged citizens of the universe. We could claim that as given by the Law: "Ye are gods; and all of you are children of the most High." (Psalms 82:6) Then we could begin to understand why the readings say that the whole answer to the world is the one ideal, "Thou shalt love the Lord thy God with all thy heart, and with all thy soul, and with all thy mind . . . And . . . Thou shalt love thy neighbor as thyself." (Matthew 22:36—40)

PART TWO
THE MODEL

Chapter Five

A MODEL FOR UNDERSTANDING THE NATURE OF MAN

From the viewpoint of the Edgar Cayce readings, *the greater study of self* should be the major project of individuals, groups, classes, and nations. We can love fully neither God nor our fellowman without a deeper understanding of ourselves. In the readings, we find an understanding of the nature of man that is equalled in few other places, either in depth or in beauty.

A proper understanding of ourselves must be built on a solid foundation. We must start with assumptions with which we are comfortable and to which we are committed. For any system of thought, the assumptions upon which it is based can never be proved; however, subsequent observations should provide confirmation.

The primary premise of the Edgar Cayce readings is *the oneness of all force.* The One Force is the Spirit of God and all that we know or experience is a manifestation of that force. A second premise is that we, all mankind, are children of God and thus spiritual beings. A third given is that the primary condition of being is consciousness and, as a corollary to this, that we are presently projecting into a three-dimensional consciousness.

There are many other dimensions in reality; however, since we are in a three-dimensional experience, it is fruitful for us to try to understand reality in terms of three-dimensional, or triune, concepts. For example, we may work meaningfully with the premise that God is one; however, we may more deeply understand His nature by working with the triune concepts of Father,

Son, and Holy Spirit. As children of God, made in His image, we are likewise aided in a better understanding of ourselves by seeing the same triune pattern of Father, Son, and Holy Spirit within ourselves as physical, mental, and spiritual beings.

Model from a Dream

Using a model as a framework for our thinking can afford us an invaluable tool. The purposes of a model are to help us organize what we already know, to help us see new relationships, and to keep us from being dazzled by the full-blown complexity of the subject matter. A model is *not* intended to be a picture of reality but a tool for thinking.

Here is a model based on a dream of Edgar Cayce. He saw himself at first as a tiny grain of sand and then, with a growing expansion of consciousness, as a spiral, a cone, a funnel opening out, as it were, from the finite to the infinite as a "trumpet of the universe" opening "an access to the Thrones themselves." In the interpretation of this dream, the source said the following should be a helpful illustration.

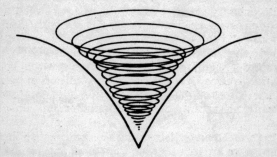

Now, let us try to deploy this model in a effort to come to a better understanding of the varied experiences with which we may become concerned in the study of self.

We may visualize man, then, primarily as a point of

consciousness which may focus on the finite or which may become attuned to the infinite. And let us visualize a model which shows the oneness in the triune. There is perhaps no more suitable three-dimensional representation of the relationship between the infinite and the finite, defining the nature of man, than is found in a cone or funnel.

In the beginning as spiritual beings, we were in the mind of God as focal points of individual awareness, yet with an open access to the infinite. The fall in the spiritual plane may be seen as a movement away from the dynamic awareness of both finite and infinite to an orientation of awareness of only the self.

Now through thoughts, experiences, and investments in consciousness, we have cut ourselves off from that immediate access to an awareness of the Divine. We may conceptualize our present levels of awareness as the consciousness, subconscious, and the superconscious potential. These are, as it were, *processes* for which there are corresponding *structures:* the physical body (conscious), the mental body (subconscious) and the spiritual body (superconscious). The spiritual body is the soul, having the attributes of Spirit, mind and will.

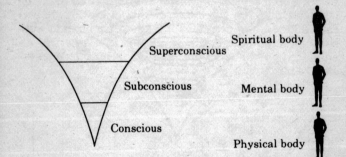

Model of the Tabernacle

According to the Cayce readings the physical body is the temple, and we may draw a direct parallel between ourselves and the construction of the Tabernacle of the Old Testament. These relationships are: the conscious and the Outer Court, the subconscious and the Holy Place, and the superconscious and the Holy of Holies.

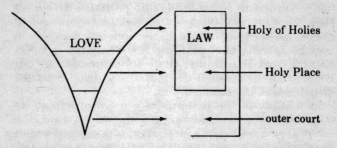

Now we may see how the ark of the covenant which contained the law and was placed in the Holy of Holies is symbolic of that law written within the depths of our own inner being. This pattern is not only the image of God but also that through which the Spirit may be given full expression in our own awareness.

We are told that at the moment of the death of Jesus on the cross, the veil in the temple was rent. This may be interpreted psychologically to mean that with the completion of His living out the life of love, there was established a new access *within us*—remember, all subconscious minds are in contact with one another—an enhanced possibility of the Spirit given renewed expression in our own lives.

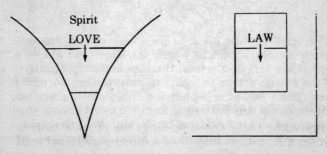

Model for Karma and Grace

When we turn away from the external world toward an awareness of our inner processes, we confront the subconscious in many forms and patterns. These are both our own creations from personal experiences and deeper patterns of the collective unconscious which may be called archetypal. Any flow of energy or information from the infinite finds its expression in our consciousness through the patterning given it by the structures of the unconscious.

In a study of the patterns of our unconscious, we may come to an understanding of the way in which the law of karma works. As a motivation is quickened within us, the life force flows through a pattern, giving expression to that motivation. This, in turn, is manifested in our external behavior as a talent, a quality of personality, a habit, or a disease. When we experience the manifestation of such patterns, we call it karma.

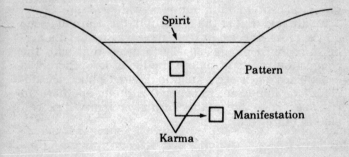

Because we were made in the image of God, there is also a pattern within us which is perfect and whole. If God is law and God is love, then the archetypal pattern of the Divine within is a pattern manifesting the life of love. Then the *law*, which the Bible says is written within us, *is* this pattern of love. When we choose this pattern as an ideal and awaken it, with both the choice of the will and the imaginative forces of the mind, we become a channel for the highest purpose of the life force. In turn, any and all karmic patterns in the subconscious may be mobilized as the stepping-stones for learning and service instead of as stumbling blocks of karma.

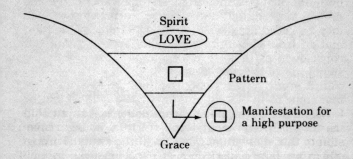

Let us consider, for example, the story of the stage magician who visited hospitalized and institutionalized young people, entertaining them with feats of magic and closing by affirming the meaningfulness of life in the spirit. It might be possible in one incarnation to develop an extraordinary talent such as special finger dexterity and utilizing that talent for negative purposes such as picking pockets. Conversely, such a talent, or karmic pattern, could be subsequently utilized for selfless purposes, as was the case of the talented magician. Mobilized for the purpose of service, this talent becomes a stepping-stone, and through this example, we may understand how we "meet" our karma yet move from karma to grace.

Model for Reincarnation

Let us consider the relationships between the physical body, mental body, spiritual body, and the conscious, subconscious and superconscious as applied to the processes of reincarnation.

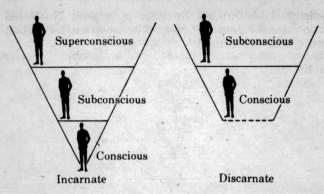

When our physical body (consciousness) is put aside as in death, our mental and spiritual bodies remain intact as the essential qualities of the entity. Through them we have experiences or consciousness in what otherwise are the subconscious and superconscious dimensions.

Later, when there is the appropriate opportunity for an incarnation, the spiritual and mental bodies are projected again into an infant body which has all the attributes for meshing the spiritual and mental patterns of the entity with an appropriate physical vehicle. Then the physical truly becomes the manifestation of the mental and the spiritual bodies. Just as a teaspoon of sugar or salt is dissolved in a glass of water—the water being the vehicle for the substance—just so does the physical body take on the distinctive flavor of that soul which has been drawn into it.

Model for Psychic and Religious Experiences

Although we have conceptualized three bodies, there is truly only one. The principle of oneness requires that the activities of the spiritual body and the mental body be reflected in the physical body. And so, at the level of the physical body, conscious processes are experienced through the cerebrospinal system, the mental body through the autonomic nervous system, and the spiritual body through the endocrine system. Illustrated below are the points of contact between the individual entity and the infinite.

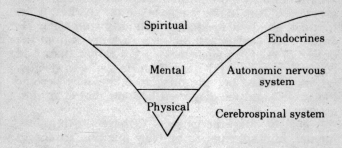

The interaction of the glands of the endocrine system and the seven spiritual centers or chakras, is the basis for understanding different kinds of psychic and religious experiences.

When we turn within, we are initially confronted by our own personal subconscious. *However, all subconscious minds are in contact with one another.* When we open ourselves without direction to these levels of consciousness, we are sensitive to or even vulnerable to the thoughts of others. As we go deeper, we find levels such as the the spirit planes and other planes of consciousness to which we may attune or which may intrude into our awareness if we are not properly directed.

Through attunement of the spiritual centers to these planes, we may communicate with discarnate entities, spirit guides, and even archangels. Our goal should always be to seek the attunement with God alone. We are to meet Him in the temple of our own bodies. If He, in turn, sends a messenger, which on occasion He surely does, that is well; however, if we seek from the outset to relate to such messengers rather than God Himself, we may receive less than He wants to give us. We may indeed become misguided, we may become idolatrous, and we may even become subject to possession.

A goal of our experience is to have the physical, mental, and spiritual to be truly one and in accord with the whole. However, these may on occasion function separately. This is sometimes an undesirable situation. The experience, which is referred to as astral projection, may be conceptualized in this model as a functioning of the mental body apart from the physical body.

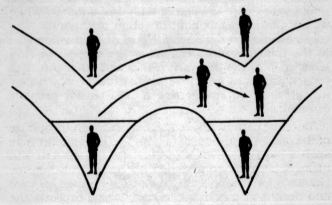

Above, two subconscious minds in contact through astral projection. Astral projection may occur as a normal part of our activities during sleep and on occasion may even be used as a modality of being of service to others. However, it must be kept in mind that our goal is to be *whole* and *one*, and to seek an integrated functioning of these structures. On one occasion when asked about his ability to conduct his work, Edgar Cayce replied that it was "the application of the harmonious triune." Oneness and attunement to the One should always be our motivation.

Model for Meditation

Meditation is attuning the physical and the mental to the spiritual. As the conscious mind is stimulated by something which may have come to it externally, such as an affirmation of love, the imaginative forces of the mind may select this same high pattern as the *ideal* to be energized by the spirit within.

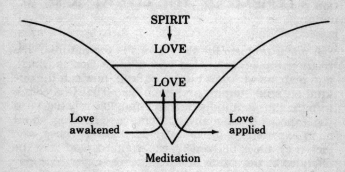

Since the pattern of love is consistent with the nature of the one force, the spirit of love, there is an affinity to such a pattern. When we attune to that pattern and make application consistent with it, we truly become channels for the Spirit. This not only brings creative and healing energy to others, but it also becomes the source of healing and transformation within ourselves.

Summary

The readings, as well as other great teachings, indicate that the greater study of mankind should be the study of self. A model, based on a dream of Edgar Cayce, has been presented. Illustrations have been given to show how the model may be employed for a better understanding of some of the major concepts and experiences in this study of ourselves. Remember the model is not a representation of reality but rather a tool to enhance deeper study of ourselves and the experiences we all encounter.

Chapter Six

THE BODY: TEMPLE OF THE LIVING GOD

A major problem for all religions is the nature of the relationship between God and man. If God is Spirit, and man, as we know him, is of flesh, how can the one kind of "stuff" impinge on the other? That God comes into the life of an individual in a tangible way has been the experience of many. Others, just hearing about such experiences, become irritated. Even those who feel they have personally experienced God may be offended by the claims of others, whose experience may differ from their own. Certainly, such visitations by the Divine remain inexplicable to most of us.

Even those who claim that God, as Spirit, can and does manifest in a tangible way in the physical, may be unable to explain how this happens or under what conditions it may occur. In all religions, the appearances of God to man have frequently seemed arbitrary and sometimes whimsical. Yet, we know that the universe is lawful, that *God is law*, and that all our experiences follow from lawful sequences of events.

How Do We Experience God in the Earth?

A slowly growing insight of man, indeed one that spans tens of thousands of years, has been that *the body is the temple* and that it is within ourselves that we meet God. One of the reasons this insight has grown so slowly is because it seems contrary to the way we experience such events. Although we may affirm that we meet God within, our experiences of the Divine may have a quality of otherness or outsideness.

The concept of projection may provide considerable help in understanding this problem. This mechanism of perception as understood by psychologists may be illustrated by the physical analogy of projection: a light passing through a slide may cast an enlarged image on a screen. The light and the slide are within but our projected experience seems to take place outside of us. For example, it is universally difficult during an ongoing dream for the dreamer not to feel that the people and events of the dream are indeed external realities rather than representations of inner processes.

When an individual has an experience of the Divine, such as a visitation by an angel, the external *otherness* of the experience may be so compelling that it seems to be entirely independent of inner processes. Because of the commanding nature of such experiences, it has taken us thousands of years to realize that all perceptions of external events are lawfully based upon internal processes. As we apply the analogy of the slide projector to our religious and mystical experiences, we gain a vivid picture of how an energy or a light, passing through the patterns or slides of the processes within our bodies, may be given a projected and enlarged representation which we experience as outside of ourselves.

Now let us address our initial question. How does the force of God, as Spirit, impinge on us as physical beings? The answer is, *from within*. The transformation of energy, from spiritual to physical, is a process that takes place within our own bodies. When Jesus said, ". . . thy faith hath made thee whole," (Matthew 9:22) He was affirming the necessity of *inner response* of the individual to the Divine within. Where this is lacking, it is said, even Jesus could do no mighty works. This is the insight contained in the expression, the body is the temple.

In the Old Testament, emphasis was given to the construction of a tabernacle or temple in which man was to meet God. The Old Testament tabernacle, with its grandeur of construction and intricacy of detail, was a *projected* enactment designed to instruct us about the nature of our own internal processes and structures.

However, even if we take this step, it is difficult to retain it for a better and more specific understanding of our own experiences, be they mystical visions, psychic awarenesses, dreams or nightmares. When such an experience occurs to us, the feeling that it is external to us is so strong—and any clues that something is occurring within us are so weak—that we fail to apply the insights we have already gained to a better understanding of such experiences.

Let us consider an example. Suppose in a dream an angel or a discarnate entity appears and gives information of a precognitive nature about some upcoming event. Following such an experience, the dreamer often insists upon being puzzled by the arbitrary nature of the visitation. Why did the vision come to me? The dreamer might more profitably ask, What is it within me that enables me to have such perceptions of the future? What is the inner process which enables there to be this momentary attunement? Can this occur more frequently or even regularly? What are the most helpful applications of such an ability?

Why Do We Have Bodies?

In order to understand the body as the temple, we must be clear about why we, as spiritual beings, have and are so caught up and invested in physical bodies.

In the beginning, in our original state as spiritual beings, we were able to move through many planes of consciousness. As freewill beings and cocreators with God, we had minds with which to build, but we built thought forms and desire patterns which deviated from the Law of One. Over time these separate projections imprisoned our own consciousness. Finally, we came to a point at which we were *lost;* we lost awareness of our oneness with God and we lost our ability to move back to Him in consciousness.

This state is analogous to that of a person who, though he may have many concerns and responsibilities, walks into a movie for a moment of diversion and gets caught up in and identifies with the action on the screen. He may get so involved in the movie that it claims his entire awareness and he forgets who he is and what he was doing before he went in.

There are two major considerations related to our involvement in the earth. In a certain sense, our inhabiting the earth is both the problem and the answer; and failure to identify the distinction between the two may lead to continuing confusion about many questions that arise in our daily lives.

Let us first consider the *problem.* As spiritual beings who have moved away from awareness of our oneness with God, we came into the earth plane, found it intriguing and fascinating, and began to identify with it, as the man who entered the movie theater lost himself and forgot his troubles. This condition posed a problem to God. How could He, as a loving Father of infinite dimensions, speak to us who had invested our consciousness so exclusively to awarenesses limited to three dimensions?

This leads us to the *answer.* It became necessary to develop a statement, a manifestation, a pattern in three-dimensional expression which would be true to the laws of the third dimension and yet in accord with the pattern of the Infinite. The development of a special creation, the human body as we know it, was one of the major steps in the Divine plan to bring man back to awareness of oneness with God.

The Microcosmic—Macrocosmic Relationship

Since God's problem was to call us to remember our heritage and our oneness with Him, it was necessary for Him to develop for us an instrument of consciousness which had the potential for a vast array of experiences.

To enable us to have the full awareness of *oneness*, it was necessary that this instrument for experiences be a miniature replica of Him and thus also of the universe. With the development of the human body, the soul now had an instrument which would enable it to experience, even in the limitations of a three-dimensional awareness, its oneness with the Infinite.

The image or likeness of God implanted within us all is a pattern in the soul's mind. With the creation of the human body, we, as lost souls, now had a vehicle through which this higher soul pattern could be given living expression in our experience in the earth.

The Way Prepared by the Pattern Applied

After evolving the human body, the next step in the solution of God's problem with His wayward children culminated in the full living expression of that image or pattern of the Divine in the life of the man Jesus. It was not enough for us to have the pattern of the Divine within. We needed to see it in action. Through Him, the pattern planted within us all was now given full manifestation in a life of perfect love of God and fellowman.

In manifesting this pattern of perfection, Jesus took on all of the traditions, prejudices, negative emotions, and multitudinous thought forms of the ages which work against the full expression of the life of the Spirit. The forces working against such an expression, both in this plane and in others, were of such magnitude that it may truly be said of this unique life that He took on the sins of the world.

We may now understand how the earth experiences

may be either the entry into imprisonment or the path toward liberation. While it is true that the desires and problems of the earth plane draw us back to subsequent incarnations, it is also true that special arrangements have been made whereby the earth experience provides a very special opportunity for awakening the soul.

Because of this pattern of the Divine in the soul, the instrument of awareness provided by the body and the new accessibility to the pattern by virtue of the life of Jesus, we have, in the earth experience, a very special opportunity to grow in our awareness of God. Incarnation into flesh gives us a greater opportunity for awakening than do some other dimensions which lack this instrument for growth and awareness. Here we receive relatively immediate feedback on the consequences of our choices, activities, and relationships with others.

The Temple as a Place

If man can have a direct experience with the Divine, are there special places in which this might be more likely to occur? There are, indeed, many places in the world which are known as holy places, because manifestations of the Divine seem to occur there more frequently. But as early as the origin of the book of Deuteronomy, there has been a strong warning not to seek God outside of ourselves. Thus, we are told:

> For this commandment which I command thee this day, it is not hidden from thee, neither is it far off.
> It is not in heaven, that thou shouldest say Who shall go up for us to heaven, and bring it unto us, that we may hear it, and do it?
> Neither is it beyond the sea, that thou shouldest say, Who shall go over the sea for us, and bring it unto us, that we may hear it and do it?
> But the world is very nigh unto thee, in thy mouth, and in thy heart, that thou mayest do it.
>
> Deut. 30:11–14

This message is reiterated throughout the Old Testament and New Testament. Why are we to meet God only within? Because what is needed is not the outside experience but the transformative power of His Spirit flowing through us. The soul, that portion of our being which may be made aware of and brought in attunement with God, is within! As His children, we are spiritual beings just as He is a spiritual being. And just as our own children may be said to be flesh of our flesh, so may we, as children of God, be said to be spirit of His Spirit. The essence of our being, then, the indwelling spirit, makes of our bodies not a place of His visitation but rather of His residence.

The Revelation of John

On more than one occasion in the early years of his work, Edgar Cayce extended a surprising invitation to students of his readings. He asked them to study the Revelation of John, because patterning for the body is expressed in the visions of John. With our new understanding of *projection*, we can see more clearly how visions, such as those experienced by John, may be the projected imagery which accompany attunement processes in the body. The readings did not represent this approach as being *the* interpretation of the Revelation, but rather as *an* interpretation which could be made individually applicable. This approach to the Revelation parallels that of the great Swiss psychologist Carl Jung, in his studies of fairy tales, mythologies, and sacred literatures of the world.

As Jung came upon extensive correlations of imagery from such varied times and sources, he hypothesized that the similarities were due to the common internal makeup of man. The basic neurology of a present-day Fijian is the same as that of an ancient Norseman. Due to the physiological parallels of all mankind, he hypothesized a common mental substratum for all experiences which he called the *collective unconscious*. As he identified major themes or images that appeared in varied human experience, he identified these recurring patterns as *archetypes* of the collective unconscious.

In this context, Edgar Cayce's approach to the Revelation was to see all the visions of John as archetypes of the collective unconscious. In other words, the visions of John represented the internal processes and structures within us all, which become involved in and indeed are the instruments of attunement to the Divine within.

The Endocrine System

In the Old Testament, the psalmist marvels at how fearfully and wonderfully the body of man is made. (Ps. 139:14) Indeed, all of its processes and structures are truly amazing. Yet one of the most amazing and one of the most important is the emotional, motivational, and coordinating system of the endocrine glands. The endocrine glands are ductless, that is to say, their secretions are released directly into the blood stream. These secretions or hormones are powerful biochemical messengers which have the potential of reaching all cells in the body and modifying their functioning in a matter of seconds. The endocrine system includes seven major centers, which may function relatively independently from each other as well as in concert.

It is known that some of these glands function as emotional and motivational centers. They act especially in response to the imaginative forces of the mind. For example, when you get angry, the adrenals secrete. The activity of the gonads, the sexual glands, is directly related to sexual motivation. And everyone knows that the pituitary is the master gland of the body, its secretions having a direct and coordinating effect on all the other glands. However, it has occurred to very few to ask what emotions or motivations are related to the pituitary, in the same way that anger is related to the adrenals. In interpreting the Revelation, the seven churches may be seen as symbolic of the seven motivational centers of the endocrine system. We may infer, then, that the motivational force of the highest, or pituitary center, would be the highest form of love or the desire for integration and oneness.

The Book with Seven Seals

In the beginning chapters in the Revelation, John sees a vision of a book with seven seals. This book may be understood to be the body, inclusive of the physical, mental, and spiritual. The seven seals indicate how removed we ordinarily are from the incredible potential of these seven glands, functioning as spiritual centers. As spiritual centers, these glands are storehouses of memory for all of our previous incarnations and, in a certain sense, the history of the soul. Since they are storehouses of karmic memory, it is by the grace of God that they remain sealed until we are on the spiritual path and prepared to deal more effectively with the memories, problems, and talents which accompany their opening.

In the vision, John weeps as he realizes that no one in heaven or earth is worthy to open the seals of this book. However, there appears a Lamb, the Christ, with seven eyes, who opens the seals one by one. This sequence of events in the vision is extremely important and instructive for us in the initial stages of our spiritual awakening. The awareness that no one is worthy enough to open these seals except the Christ, should indicate to us that no attempt to open these centers, whether by drugs, hypnosis, breathing excercises, or other specialized meditation or inner awareness techniques, should be made unless the seeker has firmly set his *spiritual ideals* and is so directed by the spirit within. The seven eyes of the Lamb symbolize the seven spiritual centers. They are the organs of perception through which we may become aware of other planes and dimensions in the same way that our commonly known five senses are organs of perception of our earth experience.

Although we have learned to think of God as One or

Triune, the Revelation speaks repeatedly of the seven spirits of God. This expression suggests seven different functions of the Divine Spirit. Thus we, as children of God made in His image, contain within us the corresponding spiritual sensory centers, which give us the potential of becoming aware of the seven aspects of the Divine.

Conclusion

The body is the temple of the living God both as the place where we may meet Him and as an instrument of awareness through which we may attune to Him. As an instrument for attunement, the endocrine glands serve as points of contact between the Spirit and the body. These centers are the transformers of the One Force of Spirit into physical consciousness and manifestation. The functioning of these centers is, in turn, dependent primarily upon the quality of motivation or ideal chosen and dwelt upon by the imaginative forces of the mind.

Chapter Seven

THE MIND: THE BUILDER AND THE WAY

The spirit is the life, the mind is the builder, the physical is the result. . . .

This frequently reiterated formula from the Edgar Cayce readings may become trite from repetition; or, as a basic premise, it may become a key to understanding some of the mysteries of the universe.

"The spirit is the life" indicates that there is only one force in the universe and this force is not only the source of all life but is life itself. "The physical is the result" indicates that all we experience in the manifest universe is a projection of energies and patterns from beyond the physical. "The mind is the builder" indicates that there is a mediating process between the spiritual reality of the one force and the manifestations of that force as we experience them in our present three-dimensional consciousness.

The role of the mind, from the perspective of the Edgar Cayce readings, is tremendous. This concept is so unusual that even those of us who are the most serious students of this information may underestimate or overlook it. Why? Perhaps because of the very magnitude of the implications of such a concept. We are like the third-grader who, while struggling to perform one-digit additions and subtractions, learns the word "calculus" from a college student. This child may have absolutely no conception of the effectiveness of the calculus in solving major engineering problems. In the same way, we may learn what someone says about the power of the mind and yet have little, if any, appreciation of a statement such as that given in the Edgar Cayce readings, namely, that the mind is nearer to being limitless than anything else in the universe.

Made in His Image

The first premise upon which we must base all our understanding is the Oneness of all force. Second, we must keep in mind that we are presently working in a three-dimensional consciousness so that our understanding of the Divine and of spiritual matters is enhanced by the utilization of triune concepts.

As we contemplate the triune nature of God with respect to the assurance that we are made in His image, we may in turn ask, "What is the triune nature of our own being which corresponds to that of the Godhead?" In the Edgar Cayce readings we are invited to consider an answer to this question that is truly amazing. The implications of this answer are so profound and far-reaching that we may too quickly accept or reject them without the deep reflection warranted by an insight of such magnitude. The answer is that the Father, Son, and Holy Spirit aspects of God parallel the physical, mental, and spiritual dimensions of our own being.

The Mind of God

The part of the formula which may most easily be understood is the relationship, indeed the identity, of the Holy Spirit with the spirit within our own inner being. The relationship which may be most difficult to understand is that which parallels the Father with the body. The Father is representative of the oneness of God and thus includes the whole. In an incarnation in the earth our physical body contains within it the mental and spiritual bodies. Thus, the "body" is inclusive of the physical, mental, and spiritual and thereby represents the whole, or the oneness as of the Father.

Now the portion of the formula with which we are concerned here is the paralleling of the macrocosmic Son with that attribute within our own inner being which the readings call "the mental" or "the mind." The implications of this are far-reaching. It must be understood that the term "the mind" does not refer to the intellect as we understand it, nor does it refer to the limitations of the conscious mind. As spiritual beings, the readings define us as souls with the attributes of spirit, mind, and will. At this spiritual level, the mind is the aspect of our being which enables us to be cocreators with God. Let us consider the expression "the mind is the builder" as it relates to the macrocosmic trinity.

In the gospel of John, we are told of the vast significance of the role of the Word or the Logos aspect of God:

In the beginning was the Word, and the Word was with God, and the Word was God.

The same in the beginning with God.

All things were made by him; and without him was not anything made that was made.

John 1:1–3

And the Word was made flesh, and dwelt among us. . . .

John 1:14

Thus the creative aspect of the Divine through which everything was made is the Word or the Logos or the Christ. And this aspect of the Divine is, as it were, the *mind* of God as the builder. There are, of course, other Biblical references to the role of the Christ in the process of creation.

What does it mean to say that the Son, or the Christ, as the mind aspect of God, is the builder or the creator? Let us consider that there is only one force in the universe, which has its primary reality in the spirit plane. The material universe about us that we refer to as physical, is a projection of this one spiritual force into manifestation. The mind is the builder because it is the patterning mediator between the hidden reality of the Spirit and the manifest projection of the physical.

Let us consider an analogy to illustrate this sequence. Suppose some people came together for the purpose of educating their children in a new way. Their desire might lead to the formulation of plans to build a new school. They prepare blueprints for the design of the school, and subsequently, the school building is actually constructed. The blueprint level is that phase which mediates or is the transition between the spirit, purpose, desire, and the actual manifestation related to that desire. Just as the blueprint constitutes the pattern for the manifested building, so is our mind the builder and our thoughts the true realities which subsequently become manifested in three dimensions. To understand more accurately how the mind works as a builder, we must introduce the concept of other dimensions.

Mind and the Fourth Dimension

The fourth dimension has its reality in thoughts and ideas. The third dimension is populated by projections from four-dimensional realities into three-dimensional manifestations. All creation, as we know it, moves through this sequence of the one force of the Spirit being given direction through desire or purpose or an ideal, followed by a patterning by the mind, and manifestation in the physical. The mind, as mediator, participates both in the physical and the spiritual as indicated in the following Edgar Cayce readings:

For, the body, and its soul is hinged upon the the mental. For, in material manifestation in a three-dimensional world, mind is the builder. . . .

2850-1

Know that the soul is eternal; the mind is both physical and spiritual; the body is only temporal. . . .

1788-3

Best definition that ever may be given of fourth dimension is an idea!

364-10

With our minds, we have built what we are and what we are presently experiencing. With our minds, and by dwelling on the ideal, we are building our bodies and experiences of the future. This future includes not only our remaining days in this incarnation but also those levels of consciousness which we will experience when we are released from the earth plane.

The Mind as the Way

Now let us consider an even more challenging concept. If we are made in the image of the triune God, what is the Christ or the Son aspect of our being? The mind! Now the macrocosmic Christ is not only the builder, as the Logos, but He is also *the Way*. Just so within ourselves the Son represented by the mind which, for us as individuals, is not only the builder but also *the Way*. For each of us, that aspect of our divine and spiritual nature which corresponds with the Christ, and thus becomes the Way, is *the mind*. The pattern of the Christ is written on that part of our soul which is the mind. When we choose that pattern and awaken it, when the mind is made one with the indwelling pattern, it *becomes the Way*.

Thus, let us try to summarize and restate the condition of man: we were made in God's image. This means not only that there is a pattern of the Divine imprinted upon the soul but also that we are a miniature model of the triune God. This means that we have the opportunity to be cocreators with Him through the Logos or Christ within—the mind. The mind is the mediator between the spiritual and the physical. We are destined to be conformed to His image but we are enabled to do that only as *we choose* that pattern as the ideal, dwell upon it with the mind, and manifest it in our lives.

Salvation is not an external event bestowed upon us, but an internal process of transformation. The atonement, or at-one-ment, is processed into our bodies and our souls by the builder and mediator—the Christ within—the mind. We are given the power and the pattern for that transformation, but we must choose the pattern, dwell upon it, and act upon it if the power is to flow through and transform us. We permit or allow His Power to transform us only through dwelling upon loving thoughts and acting in loving ways toward God and fellowman.

The Macrocosmic and the Microcosmic

Since ". . . the body and its soul is hinged upon the mental . . ." (2850–1), it is of the utmost importance that we understand the role and function of the mind. What is it and how does it work?

The physical universe about us seems so vast, real, and stable that it is almost impossible for us to conceive of an act of creation in which, by thought, there was a movement from pure energy into manifestation of the entire physical universe. It is even more difficult for us to imagine how the Creator of a universe of such magnitude could be equated with an *identity* in the way the first verses of John indicate that all that was made was made through Him, and He became flesh and dwelt among us.

The Edgar Cayce readings express the same concept, sometimes in unusual terms such as, "Who was the greatest: He who made the worlds or He who washed His disciples' feet?" Thus we find this information not only supporting and reiterating the Oneness of the Spirit manifesting in the life of Jesus and the Spirit through which the worlds were created, but also a far more difficult challenge: We, as children of God and brothers of this Son, are joint heirs in this sonship of the Divine and are indeed purposed to be cocreators with Him. Thus, the potential power of our own minds is so vast that it remains essentially unthinkable and, therefore, unexplored by us in our ordinary consciousness. There is nothing in the universe nearer to limitlessness than the mind of man.

The Microcosmic Pattern

We have previously suggested a model for understanding the nature of man in which the primary dimension of being—consciousness—is depicted as a cone. This funnel-shaped model indicates the potentials of man to both focus on the finite and to have access to the Infinite. We have suggested that we are cut off from God by barriers of our own making. We may conceptualize our present separated levels of awareness as conscious, subconscious, and superconscious. Along with these *processes*, we have also indicated parallel *structures*, namely the physical body, the mental body, and the soul or spiritual body.

Furthermore, we have indicated the following relationships in the physical body: the conscious is related to the sensory system, the subconscious to the autonomic nervous system, and the superconscious to the endocrine system. Remember, as we have developed this special concept of the mind, we have stressed that by the mind we are referring neither to the intellect nor to the conscious mind.

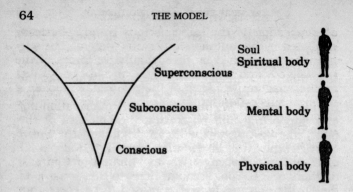

As we extend this model a step further, we come to see the special relationship between the macrocosmic trinity of Father, Son, and Holy Spirit and the microcosmic pattern of physical, mental, and spiritual.

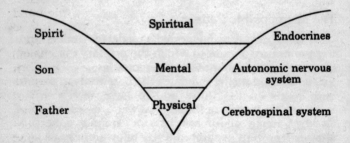

These correlations present us with the consideration of some very strange, yet very important, relationships between the subconscious processes, the mind, the mental body, the autonomic nervous system, and the Christ within. These almost unthinkable correlations may puzzle us at first; however, let us illustrate with an example from hypnosis. It is possible, with a good hypnotic subject, for the hypnotist to touch the subject with a pencil eraser, suggesting that it is a lighted cigarette, and to see an actual blister being raised on the skin. The system mediating between the verbal suggestion and the physical manifestation by the *power*

of suggestion is the subconscious mind, physically mediated by the autonomic nervous system. The suggestion is patterned by the imaginative forces of the mental body and manifested in the physical body. Just as the imaginative forces of the mind may mediate a physical suggestion into a physical manifestation, the mind may also mediate between the flow of energy from the Spirit into manifestation in our own physical bodies, as in spiritual healing.

The Power of the Mind:
Spiritual or Occult?

As we begin to study the phenomena of psychical research or, in Biblical terms, the miracles, we observe occasions when the flow of this force extends through and beyond the individual body. Prayer, distant healing, psychokinesis, and the power of projected thought in its various forms are all examples of how the mind may mediate, transform, and project the One force so as to impact on physical things at a distance.

As spiritual beings who have free (and often rebellious) wills, we are not always properly motivated by high purposes and ideals. When the forces of the mind are projected to influence others or conditions, *without respect to spiritual purposes*, we have what the readings refer to as "occultism." There is considerable confusion about this. Some people who have discovered the power of the subconscious mind think just because it works, it might be right. Not so!

Mankind has produced a number of stories about someone receiving three wishes. Typically the recipient needs the last two wishes to get him out of the trouble caused by the first wish! The moral is that the conscious mind does not know what is best. Rather than the conscious trying to program the subconscious, the conscious should invite the superconscious to express freely its high ideals.

Remember, ". . . the key should be making, compelling, inducing, having the mind one with that which is the ideal." (262–84) The power, God, the Spirit, is love. There is within us the pattern of love. When we set that pattern as the ideal and dwell upon it with the imaginative forces of the mind as in meditation, we are transformed by and become that power and pattern. As the spirit flows through us, we are healed physically, mentally, and spiritually, and we become channels for aid and healing to others. THE MIND IS THE BUILDER AND THE WAY.

Chapter Eight

THE SOUL: GOD'S COMPANION

For what shall it profit a man, if he shall gain the whole world, and lose his own soul?

Mark 8:36

The understanding of our true selves which may be gained from the Edgar Cayce readings is exceptionally beautiful, profound, and challenging. As children of God, we are heirs both to all the dimensions of the universe and to the continuity of life. The purpose of our existence is to be companions with God. We may ask, "Why would a perfect God need companionship?" But if God is love, how could He express love other than through relationship? Further, we would expect of the God of the universe that such relationships would be infinitely manifold rather than limited to a certain number.

The soul, being Divine, participates in the most essential qualities of the Divine, which are the continuity of life and awareness. Thus the soul is a citizen of eternity not only by virtue of its destiny extending into the endless future but also with its origin deriving from the endless past. Upon hearing about reincarnation, some express concern regarding the loss of individuality—of having been "someone else" other than themselves. Yet it is only the soul which is the true bearer of our individuality. In the essence of our being as souls we are more truly ourselves than even in our present material manifestations.

As cocreators with God, we are destined to participate in ever-growing, more meaningful, fulfilling, and exciting creative expressions. Throughout the past, we have participated far more than we may imagine in the creation of who we are as well as in the awarenesses, challenges, and influences we experience about us. To what extent do we create our own environs? The readings suggest that even the positions and configurations of the planets and stars about us are witnesses to what we have done as cocreators rather than influences which determine our actions.

The soul may be defined specifically as the spiritual body. The spiritual body, as such, carries the record of all thoughts and activities of its individual experience. It may be conceptualized as an energy pattern. For example, the television waves carried from the transmitter to the receiver are formless yet filled with patterned information. They are initiated in three-dimensional expression in a television studio, transmitted as an energy pattern, and reconstituted into a manifest presentation by the television receiver. If we can imagine an energy pattern which carries information and which also exists and endures in continuity in and of its own, we would have an illustration of what it means to say that the soul is the spiritual body.

As cocreators with Him, the soul may be said to consist of spirit, mind, and will. The spirit is of the one force, the life force. With our access to this force we may give manifestation to it in creative expression. The mind is the attribute of the soul, which is the builder and thus makes us cocreators with the Father. The gift of the will is also a special attribute of the spirit, which makes us free and thus more truly heirs of the Divine nature and capable of cocreating. As cocreators with free wills, we bear a far, far greater responsibility than we ever imagine for the experiences and consciousnesses of ourselves, of our creations, and of the experiences of other souls who bear the impact of our expressions.

Let us consider our proper work as souls in terms of attributes of the soul. We have defined the soul as the spiritual body with the qualities of spirit, mind, and will. Let us examine these in turn.

Spirit

The spirit as the life force of the universe is not a neutral force but one with a quality which may best be summarized by the word "Love" in the purest form. Thus, as children of God, we have access to this life force and we give natural expression to it through harmonious acts of creativity and relationship, or we may choose to deflect and color its expression by our lower, self-oriented desires and choices. The one great step in dealing with this problem of choice, which is given in the readings and which we have so often reiterated, is to establish the spiritual ideal.

As we attune ourselves to the One Spirit and as we give expression to this force in our lives, a consideration of utmost importance is the quality of purpose or intent which gives impetus to such expressions. Ultimate on the agenda of all souls is pure love of God and fellowman. This orientation toward the universal whole opposes the self-centered spirit of rebellion. The spirit of love is affirmed most clearly in the adoption of an ideal of the spirit of obedience to the higher law and the greater good.

Mind

The mind is the attribute of the soul which builds from impulse toward manifestation. As cocreators with God, we have been given that creative quality of the Divine which makes what we *think* happen. Thoughts are things, and that upon which we dwell we build not only into our bodies but also into our souls.

Furthermore, our thoughts impact on the lives of others, not only in prayer but also in mental telepathy. With every thought we think, we are either helping or hurting, aiding or hindering the person to whom or about whom the thought is directed. With the cumulative effect of our repeated thought patterns, we build thought forms which actually stand between ourselves and our attunement with others; and our impact on others is more powerful than we may ever suspect. Therefore, we must not only try to understand the power of the mind, but we must also assume responsibility for its effect; and we must with great diligence utilize this ability to pattern and direct energy only for constructive purposes. It is only when we have taken charge of our thoughts and given them positive direction, that we achieve a major step in our soul development.

Will

The most significant aspect of our opportunity for soul development in the earth plane is in the utilization of that faculty of the soul called will. The readings indicate that in the earth plane, will is the educative factor. The use of will in accord with the Law of Love teaches us attunement and provides joy, happiness, and peace. The abuse of will compels us to deal with more difficult and challenging lessons.

In spite of the great interest in the concept of free will and innumerable conversations about it, most people seem still to have little awareness of the magnitude of this gift. Our greatest personal asset is the proper use of this power so that our choices may change the circumstances, directions, and outcomes of events in our lives for the better. The readings say that no influence, whether hereditary, karmic, or otherwise, can stand in the way of the will provided that it is made one with the resident pattern of the Divine. That is to say, when we tap into the flow of this living and creative energy, we can actually change things from the course set by any predetermining influences.

A major problem for us as souls is that the mind and the will are in direct contention. With the mind we build desire patterns, thought forms, habits, obsessions, and addictions. The will remains free from these as determinants. However, they stand in a circle about the will as it is confronted with a choice, and they constitute such conveniently prepared patterns of expressions that we may give way to them as impulses, instead of using the will to be truly free.

The way to deal with this problem is to set the spiritual ideal and to give such prominence and preeminence to this ideal that it becomes the dominant factor in our motivations and the criterion for decisions at every choice point. When we make our choices on the basis of the motivating spirit of the ideal, we become free indeed.

Why Are We Here?

Before our entry into the earth plane, there were already problems. The readings clearly articulate a condition which is referred to several times in the Bible in which man, though perfect from the beginning, found within himself a spirit of rebellion. The fall, the separation, was in "heaven" or the spirit plane. It was not intended by God. It was a freewill choice.

It would be presumptuous of us to think that because of our rebellion, we will somehow come out better than those who remained in at-one-ment. Yet in spite of the pain and suffering we see about us and experience in our own lives, we still refuse to admit that something went wrong and that as spiritual beings we are individually responsible for our own separation from God. To this very moment, we continue this relative separation by our daily choices.

We have no idea how many billions of souls may have participated in this rebellion or what percentage of souls remained in harmony with God. In considering this question, we may borrow from Jesus' parable of the good shepherd. There were ninety-nine sheep in the fold and one lost. Perhaps only one percent of God's children rebelled and they are all making their way back.

The readings say that there is soul entrapment throughout the universe. Therefore, those fallen are not limited just to the souls presently working in our solar system. At the level of the spirit plane, or mental plane, some souls who have separated themselves from the Whole are not even aware of their separation.

If there is soul entrapment throughout the universe, we in this system may be in an exceptionally fortunate position. Being able to incarnate in the earth plane is a special opportunity to gain a growing awareness of the consequences of our thoughts, choices, and actions. It provides unique opportunities to remember who we are and to grow in attunement with God.

More importantly, an event has taken place in the life of this solar system in the past two thousand years in the birth, life, death, resurrection, and continuing work of the spirit of Jesus of Nazareth which gives all souls in this system a pattern of approach, a new access to energy and a new awareness of the love of God. Thus He has given us hopefulness of inestimable value. As in the parable of the good shepherd who set out to find the lost sheep, so God, as our Father, has sent the Christ to help us find our way back to oneness with Him.

The readings say that nothing more true has ever been expressed than God's unwillingness that any soul should perish. No matter how we fall, He continues to provide a way by which each of us may move in consciousness from whatever state we may find ourselves through a growing awareness, until we are again fully at one with Him.

Being in the earth plane is not only an opportunity to view the consequences of our actions and thoughts, but it is also like the play area of a school. There are toys with which we may play, but we also have the opportunity to outgrow these earthly experiences, emotions, and possessions in an ever-increasing awareness that these toys and experiences do not fulfill our soul's real longing and desires. We yearn to return to our true home and to participate in its proper cosmic realm of activity.

Thus we are here, as indicated in the parable of the prodigal son, not only because we have gone astray of our own choice but, more importantly, because we need to have the opportunity to remember who we are, to awaken to ourselves, and to arise and return to our Father.

It is said that God created man in His image; more specifically it is the soul that is created in the image of God. Thus, the soul possesses all the attributes and aspects of the nature of the Divine. To say that we are made in His image indicates that no matter how far astray we may go, there still remains within us the pattern of and the link to perfection through which we may regain full attunement with the Whole.

How Does It Work?

The soul, as a spiritual body, is not only a cocreator with God, but it also bears the records of all our thoughts and activities. Thus there are emanations from our thoughts and activities which are recorded on the soul in God's Book of Remembrance, sometimes referred to as the Akashic records. These impressions, recorded on the skein of time and space, may be read on occasion by one such as Edgar Cayce, who could put his lower self aside so completely as to make attunement with the Infinite, seeking that which would be helpful and hopeful for the individual whom he would serve. Each of us may attain to that state in which the Spirit will bring all to our remembrance; and we, too, will have a personal awareness of these records.

The soul incarnates into the physical body at or about the time of birth. Sometimes the first breath of the infant body is accompanied by the entrance of the soul. Much preparation will have preceded this event. Many choices are made at the soul level of the entities involved. The soul pattern or purposes and lessons to be learned throughout successive incarnations become predisposing factors for the projected circumstances of the incoming entity. The ideals and purposes of the parents, which are uppermost in their minds at the time of conception, become especially important influences which attract a soul to a specific body.

Remember, the soul not only bears the records of the individual, but it is also an energy pattern. The emanations from the records of the soul quickly permeate every cell of the physical body and it thus becomes truly and uniquely an appropriate expression of that soul with respect to the purposes, relationships, and experiences to be dealt with in that incarnation.

No matter what others may say, we should not get the idea that we are only "half" of a soul and not complete until we find our soul mate. Nor should we entertain ideas that the soul is manifesting in several other bodies at the same time and thus not giving full attention to the task at hand. It is also useless to think that part of the soul is working on several other incarnations in time periods other than the present. Remember, one soul for every body, and one body for every soul incarnate in the earth.

One Life to Live?

The perspective of our present consciousness in which we feel we have only one life to live, may seem—especially when we are in pain and suffering—interminable and of all-surpassing importance. True, life is earnest and the stakes are high. But souls have been in the earth plane for millions of years. So, seventy or eighty years of great suffering, if used to learn a great lesson or to meet a severe challenge, to fulfill a great responsibility or to maintain a self-sacrificing integrity to make possible a life of service, does not seem so overwhelming or burdensome to the soul. Our limited and finite consciousnesses only are overwhelmed and tried.

We Are Unique

In the creation of souls, God did not stamp out an infinite number of us, as if on an assembly line. On the contrary, each was created with special and unique individual qualities, none less valuable in the eyes of God than another. Thus each of us has a special job to perform—even in our present relatively finite and limited relationships and understandings—that can be done by no other soul. If we can adequately estimate the enormity of this truth, then we can understand when the readings say to each of us that God not only created us to be companions with Him but that He is lonely without us.

Other Life Forms

Of all the forms of life in the earth plane, only man is a manifestation of this special gift of the Divine, the soul. Many of us who are lovers of animals or of special pets, may feel that these beings are unique individuals who not only come to us from previous life experiences, but who are also deserving of an opportunity to evolve in the future. It is true, there have been many experiences which suggest the continuity of the personality of animals. Some of these experiences relate to previous lives and others to continuity of existence beyond physical death of the animal. However, we should understand this continuity as expressions of the mental body or the astral body of the animal and not of any Immortal soul quality.

A fuller understanding of ourselves as cocreators, capable of projecting thought forms which may demonstrate a considerable measure of autonomy, will be very helpful to a better understanding of our relationship to special animals. Even though we may experience an animal as having a continuing identity over time, such experience may be more *our* awareness of relationships

to aspects of ourselves than to the individuality of the
animal, just as we project aspects of ourselves onto
other people.

For example, a man may have a dog which he experiences as having a personality of its own; however, it
may also be observed that there is a marked relationship or similarity between the dog's personality to that
of its owner. As we observe this, we come to see how
some of the personality of the animal may well be the
thought form projection of the owner. A pet may even
take on the neuroses of its owner! Now we may understand how such thought forms could even seem to
"reincarnate" from one animal to another.

Thus it is all the more important, if we are truly
concerned about our beloved animal friends, that we
dedicate our efforts to the healing of our wayward souls
and those of our fellowman. For only as mankind is
made whole, may the animal kingdoms manifest their
own aspects of the Spirit, unhindered by our projections.

Summary

We are souls, spiritual beings who have created for
ourselves mental bodies and are projecting into physical bodies. There is a portion of us, the spirit entity,
which is perfect and has never left the throne of God.
Thus there is the potential—called the superconscious—
for the soul to be in attunement with the Whole. But
there is a portion of us born of a spirit of rebellion
which has gone its own willful way. Thus we find ourselves in the present finite physical consciousness. The
readings describe this as a condition in which the soul
slumbers and "dreams," and participates in a finite
and limited consciousness. However, the soul is judged
by choices which it makes in these "dreams," during
periods of seeming wakefulness.

In terms of our considerations of the nature of the
soul, we may delineate the steps of soul development
very succinctly. We must set a spiritual ideal—ultimately
there is only one, love of God and fellow souls—requiring

our minds to dwell upon the ideal, and make and act upon choices which are motivated and measured by that ideal. Then the mind and the will can be brought into harmony with the spirit; and we become free to express, each in his own unique way, our love of God and man.

PART THREE
THE LAWS

Chapter Nine

ONENESS AND LOVE

The reiterated first premise given throughout the Edgar Cayce readings is the *oneness of all force*. This is a basis upon which all subsequent understanding may develop, and it is a point to which we will undoubtedly return in considering and evaluating any specific direction of thought.

The oneness of all force constitutes a premise which in philosophic terms may be called monistic. As such it stands in marked contrast to forms of thought which are dualistic. Dualism assumes that there are two essential realities. Tendencies to dualism are seen in differentiations between spirit and matter, mind and body, the non-manifest and the manifest, and especially in some conceptualizations of good and evil as opposing forces. While it is very important to differentiate between the Creator and that which is created, such a distinction, essential or otherwise, may incline us to dualistic attitudes and thinking patterns.

Much theology in maintaining the distinction between the Creator and the created, and in trying to deal with the reality of evil and the lost condition of man, has unwittingly elevated the concept of evil to a first premise. Some notions of the Battle of Armaggedon in the last days see it as a showdown between the forces of Good and the forces of Evil. This dualism constitutes a most serious problem in theology as well as psychology, and it has far-reaching ramifications in our attitudes toward our fellowman and the universe.

If we think there are two forces at work in the universe, Good and Evil, and if we see these at work in the earth, then we may see our enemy aligned with the forces of evil. These attitudes may quickly betray the ideals of love of God, of neighbor, and of enemy, from the personal to the international level. Whether it be an individual committing a series of crimes of violence or vast nations, how are we to love them if we see them as our enemy? The premise of oneness, added to the reincarnation notion that we must one day meet again and make our peace with these fellow children of God, may enable us now to work with better attitudes toward all. Thus, in order to love more fully, we need a much greater consciousness of oneness.

The reality of evil, of course, must be recognized. However, this acknowledgment does not mean that evil is thereby elevated to a premise leading to a dualistic view of the universe. Yet much of the present emphasis on believing in both God and the devil is a form of idolatry contrary to the admonition of the lawgiver, "Know O Israel, the Lord Thy God is One."

A most important way of understanding the nature of evil is by recognizing that we have separated ourselves in consciousness from God. We hear of the ostrich who puts his head in the sand. It is an appropriate image, helpful in visualizing the status of man. God hasn't gone anywhere; but we have separated ourselves in consciousness from him. Since the spirit of rebellion and the consequent consciousness of separation is the problem, all dualistically inclined philosophies, no matter how high or helpful, tend to perpetuate the basic problem of separation. On the other hand, we must not deny the reality of evil, encouraging the untenable affirmation that everything is going the way it should. This type of philosophy in effect denies free will and attributes growth to evolutionary forces, maintaining that any choice we make is the right one for us at the time.

Evil is a product of rebellion, even found in us who are spiritual beings, God's own children. However, it is not an *evil force* opposed over and against a *good force*. Rather, we may say that within the being of the one God there are focal points of consciousness that have gone astray from the awareness of the oneness.

And the more surely God is omnipotent and omniscient, the more surely he longs for the return of his children who have gone astray.

Once we are clear about the monistic aspects of this premise, we can see that the mission of God, so frequently articulated in the New Testament, is not overcoming evil but rather *reconciliation* with His children. Now, with a consciousness of oneness, we have a basis upon which to take more seriously the teaching of Jesus that we are to love our enemies.

A far-reaching implication of the premise positing the oneness of all forces is that ultimately all will be brought into accord with this oneness. The implication of that for us as individual souls, children of God, is that all souls one day will be brought into oneness with Him. This suggests, of course, a theology of *universalism*, that *all* may eventually be saved. To our amazement we find that many who preach a gospel of love and salvation are nevertheless greatly distressed even to reflect upon this possibility.

Love and Law

The basic assumption of all science is lawfulness. The scientist could not proceed in his work if he did not hold this assumption. I have often thought that the atheistic scientist holds the logically untenable position of having to assume that the universe is *accidentally lawful*! But accidental assumptions do not even fit with the findings of science itself. For example, the big-bang theory of the universe includes a clear observation that chemical combinations that develop are not random but follow preferred pathways for the formation of certain compounds.

There is an intrinsic relationship between law and good. While many people are prepared to say that the universe operates lawfully, they may not see the implication that this lawfulness means there is an essential *goodness* about it. Many say the law is neutral; yet, if in its operations it were not lawful, we would surely say, "That's bad!" For example, if we were to plant a tomato seed and it was to grow up to be a weed, we would be greatly distressed and we would say, "That is not good." If we were to anticipate a warm day in midsummer and suddenly there were a great blizzard, we would say, "That is not good." And so we come to depend upon the sun rising in the east and setting in the west, the cycle of the seasons, and the lawfulness of life about us. All of these lawful manifestations imply a *goodness*. In the greatest sense, then, we may say there is lawful *cosmos* which is good instead of unlawful *chaos* which we would surely experience as being bad.

This attitude, this premise that that which is lawful is therefore good, should be richly applicable for us as an attitude about all that we meet, experience, and observe in life. If we would see the manifestations in our own lives and in those about us as being lawful and therefore good, in contrast to being unlawful, we would be close to loving God, because part of loving God is loving that which is lawful and sensing that it is good.

The Nature of the One Force

As we come to understand the relationships between law and good and between good and love, we may sense that the one force is not a neutral force, certainly not a bad force, but rather a force that has the essential quality of being good. Because there is life, there is a special quality of this energy that brings forth experiences, growth, and transformation. Behind this there must be some extraordinary intelligence! In the manifestations of life through the light of this Intelligent Creator, we may see that His Beingness is Love. Even in the physics of an atom or a solar system we may see a quality that may be instructive for us in understanding the *physics of love* in the universe. There is a law of attraction and a law of repulsion, and there is a balance that is maintained between the two. How can such forces be observed in the atom and in the solar system? If there were only attraction, an atom or a solar system would collapse in on itself. If there were only repulsion there would be no integrative systems. Observing the balance of these systems, we may learn something about the physics of love that holds things together, yet maintains them at a distance in which there can be individualities and thereby living processes and relationships.

Once we are prepared to seriously address the patent intelligence manifested in creation, we can sense the Beingness behind it all. For the finite mind to dismiss out of hand because it cannot conceptualize, is like an ant not "believing in" man because it can not comprehend. The concept of the oneness of all force may become the basis for sensing a personal relationship to the universe that is far deeper and richer than, say, imagining either an old man with long gray hair we call God, or a neutral universe that has a cold and impersonal quality about it.

As we begin to work with the premise of oneness, we may begin to see a oneness manifested in things about us. Holographic photography has taught us a lesson that the whole pattern may be contained in a fractional part. Thus, we should not be surprised, as we consider the principle of oneness, that one sample may reveal much of the pattern of the whole. Whether it is the date of birth, the numerology of a name, the graphology of handwriting, the physiognomy of the face, a voice analysis, a drop of blood or the genetic code in a single cell, we may find in all of these peripheral perspectives that which gives us a picture of the whole individual. We should also understand that these are only outward signs, perhaps leading to a deeper consideration of the integrity and oneness of each unique individual as a spiritual being.

Oneness as Consciousness

When the Edgar Cayce readings tell us that the first lesson for six months should be oneness, oneness,

oneness, then we may address oneness as an attitude or consciousness. The consciousness of the oneness of all force is not the same as the consciousness of a *one thing*. Since we are in three dimensions and are oriented toward things, when we hear the word one, we may think of one thing. This has been part of the problem in attempting to address the reality of God. But if we bring the oneness of all force to bear on this consideration, as a principle, then we may see that oneness does not imply a one thing. Therefore, we can apply this principle of oneness to God without implying that He is in a one place somewhere out there.

The consciousness of the oneness becomes the basis of love. Oneness is a way of defining the Christ consciousness, which is the awareness of the oneness of the soul with God. He who said, "I and the Father are one," also said, "I in you and you in me," pursuing an attempt to develop within us this awareness of the oneness. Oneness as consciousness implies a special kind of interrelationship among all things. We must bring this consciousness to bear on our attitudes toward other peoples, other nations, the ecology, the heavens themselves. As a working principle, Oneness reveals our deep need to change our attitudes and the effects these have upon our behaviour towards others and the world about us.

The Great Commandment

It is only with the consciousness of the oneness of all force that we can begin to take the great commandment as seriously as we should. The great commandment is the commandment of love. It is the commandment to love all without exception. It becomes a basis from which to formulate our attitudes toward all considerations. We should continue to ask, however, why it is that there are two aspects to the great commandment. We are told we must both love God with all our heart, mind, and soul, and our neighbor as ourselves. Love of God is our orientation toward Reality, toward the Law, toward the Universe, and it indicates our desire to be in at-onement with and in accord with Reality, with the Truth, with the way things are, with the ultimate Light and Life and Love which are the essential qualities of the universe.

On the other hand, to love our neighbor is to recognize the *oneness* even where there are differences between us. It may help to reflect again upon the fact that God made as many of us as He did; it seems to imply that He loves variety. We have only to look at the vast number of species of plants, of birds, of fish, and of other aspects of creation to sense that oneness is found in the interrelationships and interdependencies of patterns rather than in a singleness of pattern. Therefore, as we seek to love our neighbor and sense a quality of oneness in that relationship, we may come to respect, perhaps value, and perhaps even to love the difference this or that neighbor embodies. And we may see how it may enrich our own lives as we, cocreators, share one another's differences, further stimulating each other's consciousness.

All souls in the universe must one day or one eon be brought into accord with the law of love. We were created in the image of love; it is our destiny to be conformed to that image. We as spiritual beings, possessing free will, must one day manifest that accord through using our free will and cocreativity in total accord with the great commandment. We must one day come to love God with all our heart, mind, and soul. Our neighbor must be defined as one who is in need and so our love must, of necessity, come to include those whom we presently call our enemies.

The Edgar Cayce readings, in presenting the great commandment as the answer to the world, say that while we must have the same *ideal*, we cannot have the same *idea*. The more we reflect upon the difference between ideas and ideals, the more helpful and instructive we may find it to be. Again and again we find ourselves differing in ideas, often permitting that difference to separate us from pursuing a work together on the basis of a shared ideal. We feel that to be in accord we must have the same idea. But not only is this often unnecessary, in many cases it is not even desirable. The richness of individual souls prohibits us from ever having precisely the same ideas. We can come to value, respect, and even love that quality of uniqueness. Then these differences become enriching rather than disappointing, encouraging us to share the one ideal.

The Law of One

Having established oneness as a first premise, we may put ourselves in accord with a work that has its origins in the prehistoric past. We are told in the Edgar Cayce readings of a work developed more than twelve thousand years ago that was called "the law of one." When this "law of one" was brought to bear on conditions facing the people of that time, we find that new attitudes were developed toward the races, the sexes, and the many different types of beings through which souls were incarnating. The "law of one" brought about a whole new order and a new age.

Those of us who align ourselves with this premise today may again begin to contribute in an extraordinary and helpful way toward bringing about a new age in our time, a new consciousness that embraces all persons as fellow children of God. We may begin and help develop a consciousness that concerns itself with the oneness of the world and sets about to build a oneness in interpersonal, national, and international relationships. This marvelous and beautiful living sphere, the planet earth, cries out for such a consciousness.

Oneness and Integration

The psychology of oneness is a call to the individual to integration within his own being. We are not whole psychologically or physically because we are not in at-one-ment in our inner selves. As we set about becoming integrated or becoming whole, we may first remember that the most important experience for all is to know what is the ideal spiritually. If, in setting a spiritual ideal, we can guide our motivational potentials toward a singleness of purpose, then we may begin to experience the statement of Jesus that, if your eye be single, the whole body may be full of light. If the eye is single, that is to say, if within ourselves we are single or one in purpose, then physically, mentally, and spiritually we may be filled with light.

The principle of oneness is behind the practice of meditation as we seek attunement, atonement, and at-one-ment within. The spirit of oneness requires a spirit of forgiveness because there can be no oneness either within ourselves or in our relationships with others unless we forgive. The spirit of oneness requires that there be a coming together of the forces within ourselves. In this process we may have our own body filled both with light and become a light unto the world.

Chapter Ten

TIME, SPACE, AND PATIENCE

In the Edgar Cayce readings we are told that the first premise is the Oneness of all force. This is an essential concept for us to understand. There is only One Force in all the universe. That Force is not neutral; it is the Spirit; it is the Life Force. It is Love. It is Law. It is God. We and all that we experience about us are manifestations of that One Force.

The Edgar Cayce readings also tell us that we as spiritual beings were with God and of God from the beginning, before there was an earth and even before there was a creation, as we understand creation in a physical sense. As spiritual beings and as children of God, we were with Him and perfect in the beginning.

He created us out of his desire for companionship, and He sought that we would be cocreators with Him.

Only One Law was written by the One Force: to love thy Lord, thy God, with all thy heart, and thy mind, and thy body, and thy neighbor as thyself. Perfect though we were, there arose within some of us, in some inexplicable way, a spirit of rebellion, an urge to break that Law. This rebellion became an expression of selfishness, rejecting a sustained awareness and consideration of the greater good of the Whole. There was no need for going astray, but we fell!

The question is always asked. "How could a perfect being fall?" Since it is we who fell, we can answer that within ourselves because to this day we still carry that spirit of rebellion within us. We need to look no further than the daily confrontation between what we know we should do, and what we want to do. The fall was a spiritual fall, and occurred within the spirit realm. It had nothing to do with our appearance in the earth plane nor with the attractions of the flesh. These came much later.

It is still widely thought that our experience in the earth plane is an undesirable consequence of or punishment for the fall. The readings indicate, however, that we should view our incarnations as opportunities for constructive self-development.

As we examine the readings more carefully, we learn that the development of materiality and our experience of consciousness in this plane were necessary. Those of us who had fallen and become so enmeshed in our own thought forms needed an awareness of our separation from the One. In fact, we did not even know that we had become separated, so caught up were we in our own creations. In meeting ourselves in these earth plane manifestations which we had built, we had the opportunity to sense our separation from God, and to perceive God's invitation to return to a full and harmonious awareness of our oneness with the Whole.

The readings indicate that God has prepared an

almost infinite array of opportunities and dimensions to meet the individual requirements of each soul to find its way of return.

> For it is not the will of God that any soul perishes, but with every temptation, with every trial there is prepared the way of escape.
>
>   5755–2

And so, although we may permit ourselves to become enmeshed and lost in our experience in the earth plane, its purpose is rather an awakening and purification, an opportunity presented by the Father Himself as preparation for our return to Him.

Three Dimensions

Now we have come to understand that the nature of our present consciousness is three-dimensional, and that the very characteristics of our present plane of awareness are such that we are in a three-dimensional experience. We speak of the Father, the Son, and the Holy Spirit, and yet we know there is only One God; we speak of Oneness in truine terms simply as a way to better comprehend Oneness with our finite minds.

What are these dimensions of our experience? Two of them we can name with some agreement, even certainty. It is clear to all of us that *Time* is a way of measuring or characterizing our experience, our awareness, our learning, and our growth. Second, it is also clear that *Space* is a dimension of our common experience. It is the beingness of the physical universe about us and of its manifestations. Space is the arena in which we conduct our experiences in time.

Beyond time and space we all sense that there is a greater and even more important dimension to our common experience. The Edgar Cayce readings define this third dimension as *Patience*.

All who are familiar with the Bible have heard the patience of Job extolled. We know that patience is one of the fruits of the Spirit. Yet we might wonder how patience can be a dimension. Let us consider for a moment that *a dimension is a mode of measurement.* We measure our lives in terms of Time, in terms of Space, and with respect to the soul's growth, we measure our lives in terms of Patience.

Let us examine this more closely. In Space, as in the manifestations in nature, we see the hand of God at work in a beautiful flower, in a sunset, in all of creation. In Time, as in growth and change, we see the hand of God at work in the seasons, in night and day, in the cycle of the seed as it falls into the ground, dies, comes to new life, and bears fruit in its season. In the acts of man, the essential quality of the fruit of the Spirit is Patience. Patience, thus, becomes a measure of our full and abiding attunement with the Spirit, the Oneness.

Now we are challenged to take our understanding one step further. If there is only One Force, God, and if reality is presenting itself to us at the present in terms of the dimensions of time, space, and patience, then would it not follow that our mode of experiencing the truine God—Father, Son, and Holy Spirit—is through our own individual trinity of body, mind, and soul? As we come to see God manifested on these individual levels, we shall also understand that our experiencing of Him also occurs through the triune dimensions of time, space, and patience.

These insights may awaken within us a new and extraordinary response to the nature and purpose of the experiences in which we find ourselves. These insights should revolutionize our attitudes toward our opportunities in the earth plane. Previously, we may have felt that the earth experience was evil or that we were trapped in a lesser reality; now we may come to see that these presentations of time, space, and patience are indeed of God Himself. We experience true reality, and thus God in these dimensions, in order that we may have the opportunity to awaken, to attune, and to return. In every experience we should see Him in His love and lawfulness as presenting Himself to us for our growth. In every experience we should sense that He is presenting us with a stepping-stone rather than a stumbling block for our soul's growth.

At any time and facing any circumstance, if we are ready to grow, then that circumstance or experience can become instructive. Simply by bringing to life a willingness to grow and to learn, we meet God in all of life.

The additional ingredient needed to make sense of this perspective of life is of course *ourselves*. We are continually meeting self. Because we have minds with which to build and wills with which to choose, we can place ourselves in a certain relationship to God and to the Law. The circumstances we meet in life give testimony to what we have done or to the positions we have taken with respect to the Law.

Since there is only One Force, since God is that Oneness, and since the Divine is Infinite, then from the point of view of cosmic consciousness, there is only one time and there is only one space. For the Infinite there is no time or space as we in our finite consciousness understand them. Yet by the grace of God we are permitted to live and grow in a three–dimensional awareness; therefore, it is essential for us to understand the nature of these dimensions and to work with them. Only as we are obedient to the laws of the physical, mental, and spiritual dimensions do we become free from them.

If these dimensions are made for man's growth in awareness, how do they function in this respect? It is through the records that man himself makes, that he encounters himself in terms of the purposes, choices, and applications made with respect to the Law. Thus, it is said that "upon the skein of time and space" these records of man's experiences are written. It is only in patience that we may ultimately read and become aware of these records, but in this awareness no time and no space exist in the unity of at-one-ment.

The readings reiterate that patience is not a passive, but rather an active force. If patience is an active force, then some force must be raised within us which enables us to apply patience. In deep meditation we may raise the spiritual forces within the body and these forces may flow through the seven spiritual centers of the body. Thus, if patience is an active force to be applied, and if the life force is raised in and through us in deep meditation, then it follows that in order to be patient we need to become meditators!

In seeking to apply patience, there may be misunderstandings. Many people erroneously think that patience will make them a kind of doormat or lessen their strength of character. The readings correct this misconception many times. For example:

To be sure patience, long-suffering, and endurance are, in their respective manners, urges that would lead to virtues, but they cease to be a virtue when the individual entity allows self merely to be imposed upon, and to take second place merely because someone else of a more aggressive nature, imposes.

3029–1

For each of us, each soul, patience is the lesson we must learn during our sojourn through materiality. It is in and through patience that man becomes more and more aware of the continuity of life and of his soul being a portion of the Whole. Time and space are the dimensions through which we come to understand the creative and motivational forces, while patience reveals man's response to God and what we have done in our relationship to Him.

Chapter Eleven
KARMA AND GRACE

Reincarnation is an immediate and natural corollary of the great first premise that *God is love*. Both the continuity of the life of the souls of men, who are the children of God, and God's continuing forgiveness as the Father of His children who have gone astray follow, of necessity, from the very nature of God Himself.

It would be helpful at this point to review the parable of the Good Shepherd from the New Testament.

> "How think ye? If a man have a hundred sheep, and one of them be gone astray, doth he not leave the ninety and nine, and goeth into the mountains, and seeketh that which is gone astray?
>
> "And if so be that he find it, verily I say unto you, he rejoiceth more of that sheep, than of the ninety and nine which went not astray.
>
> "Even so it is not the will of your Father which is in heaven, that one of these little ones should perish."
>
> Matthew 18:12–14

If a good shepherd would go out in active pursuit of the very last sheep, how much more would an All-Loving Father persist in active pursuit of His children down through the corridors of time into the vaults of eternity? As the parable ends with Jesus saying that it is not the will of the Father that one of these little ones should perish, so do the Edgar Cayce readings affirm that nothing truer has ever been spoken than that God is not willing for any soul to perish.

However, many who feel they have come to know God in their lives without the concept of reincarnation are fearful that this principle is contrary to what they have come to value and understand about the redeeming work of His spirit in their own lives. Rather than seeing the promise of *grace* that reincarnation offers for all mankind, they fear that the law of karma detracts from the work of Jesus and from the promise made of an immediate and exclusive place in heaven. This is due to a misunderstanding of the meanings and implications of both the law of karma and the law of grace.

A careful study of the Bible leaves us with the same problem—with or without the concept of reincarnation. On the one hand, we are told that every jot and tittle of the law must be fulfilled, that they who take the sword shall perish by the sword, and that whatsoever a man soweth, that shall he also reap. On the other hand, we are told of grace and forgiveness, of a redemptive and atoning work that we may invite into our lives. Thus, even without the concept of reincarnation, we find in the Bible some statements of the law which are not easily understood or reconciled with the concept of grace and forgiveness. We are left with a notion of a God who visits His grace and forgiveness on those of His choosing by whimsical, if not capricious, standards. Two hospital roommates die on the same day. One has a deathbed conversion and goes to an eternal heaven, the other to an eternal hell. Such a theology reflects neither law nor love. Let us reexamine, then, the nature of law which some call the *law of karma* and the nature of love which some refer to as the *law of grace.*

In Sanskrit the word *karma* means simply *action.* It is frequently referred to as the law of cause and effect. We may well modify our terminology, as science has, from the term cause and effect to the broader term antecedents and consequences. Perhaps an even better understanding of karma as a law is found in the expressions "each after its own kind" and "like begets like." Just as rabbits beget rabbits, and tomatoes beget tomatoes, so in human experience, acts of kindness beget further acts of kindness, and acts of anger beget further acts of anger.

This is a *law,* not in a moralistic or judgmental sense, but rather in the sense that it is the way things work. Thus, in considering the law of karma, let us put aside all notions of retaliation, retribution, and judgment, and let us work more simply and deeply with an appreciation of the extraordinary fineness over time of the way in which *like begets like.* Since we are co-creators with God, that which we think and experience not only happens to us, but also becomes a part of us. And since it is a part of our being, it becomes that which must be met if it stands between ourselves and our awareness of our oneness with God.

The Edgar Cayce readings, following the Bible, leave no doubt about the exactitude of this as an immutable law. "Whatsoever a man sows, that shall he also reap" is as literally true in the realm of human experience and behavior as it is in the realm of horticulture.

As we try to understand the working of the law of karma, there are several considerations to be kept in mind. One is that the patterns we build within ourselves remain without respect to time. If we reap what we sow, then some might expect a close proximity in time between the two events. However, there is a quality about the unconscious that is timeless.

It has been said that some grain seeds have been discovered in archaeological remains from ancient Egypt which may be as old as four or five thousand years. When these seeds were placed under conditions suitable for germination, they came to life even after lying dormant for centuries. So, within ourselves we may find that the seed of an attitude or action in one experience may not come to fruition until many incarnations later. Some complain that it is not fair to have to pay for something that someone else did. However, that is just the point: We are meeting *ourselves*; it was not someone else but ourselves, who in those experiences in the past established the patterns dictating the circumstances in which we find ourselves in the present.

Another aspect of this law that may not be well understood is the movement from the level of mind as the builder to the physical as the result. That which is held in one experience as an attitude or a pattern of behavior may be brought into manifestation in a subsequent incarnation as a quality of the body. Thus our present physical appearances or diseases may be the consequents of antecedent attitudes and actions.

A serious misunderstanding of the law of karma is that we are paying for some indebtedness we have incurred. It is not a matter of paying a debt, but rather of coming to grips with that which the self has built. This distinction should make a considerable difference in our attitude. One point of view suggests that an arbitrary judge is requiring payment; the other has the connotation that the karmic manifestation is the natural and lawful consequent of antecedent behavior or thought. When the karmic experience is especially painful it may be felt that there is a retributive quality to karma. But neither God nor the law are punitive or retributive; rather, that which we meet is the natural result of that which we have previously built for ourselves.

Let us consider how the readings describe the nature of the law of grace.

> For the law of the Lord is perfect, and whatsoever an entity, an individual sows, that must he reap. That as law cannot be changed. As to whether one meets it in the letter of the law or in mercy, in grace, becomes the choice of the entity. If one would have mercy, grace, love, friends, one must show self in such a manner to those with whom one becomes associated. For like begets like.
>
> There are barriers builded, yes. These may be taken away in Him, who has paid the price for thee; not of thyself but in faith, in love, in patience, in kindness, in gentleness may it be met.
>
> That these have been the experience may appear to the entity as rather unfair. Is it? The law of the Lord is perfect. His grace is sufficient, if thy patience will be sufficient also.
>
> 5001–1

The question, of course, is, "How do we move from the law of karma to the law of grace?" There are three key concepts related to this movement: setting ideals, making choices in accord with these ideals, and applying said choices.

> Thus . . . if ye live by law ye must judge by law. If ye live by faith, ye judge by faith. If ye live by grace, ye must practice grace—and be gracious. If ye would have friends, ye must show yourself friendly. If ye would have patience, ye must be patient first with self, and then with others.
>
> 2981–1

Now the question may arise as to the aspect of the law of karma that is immutable and says we must meet every jot and tittle. We must meet what we have built, but we may meet ourselves under the law of grace. Yes, what self has built must be met, but by the spirit in which we meet it we may experience an entirely different outcome. Now it may be quickly said, as we are instructed from the Bible, that grace is a gift of God and freely bestowed. However, it is not bestowed whimsically, but lawfully. If we would have grace, we must be gracious. Thus the Master taught us to pray, "Forgive us our debts, as we forgive our debtors." Our constant prayer, then, is to be forgiven to the extent that we forgive.

Now we may introduce another principle of the law of karma: like begets like. This law refers to *quality*, but not necessarily to *quantity*. If we make a hundred mistakes of the same kind, it does not necessarily mean that we must meet this condition a hundred more times with a better response. Just as a kernel of corn may bring forth a hundredfold, the law of karma says that corn will produce corn, but not how much! If we plant forgiveness, we may reap forgiveness a hundredfold. It is not that God thinks of mankind as debtors who must pay, but rather as His children who need to learn the law of love.

Now let us consider the relationship of the law of karma and the law of love from another perspective. Remember the formula from the readings which says, "The spirit is the life, mind is the builder, and the physical is the result." Let us consider this formula in terms of the following relationship.

Since mind is the builder and the physical is the result, then that which is built as karma resides as a pattern in the mind, which one day may be brought into manifestation in the physical. On occasion, the readings refer to karma as simply giving way to impulse. It is as though there may be a pattern in the mind which need not be given expression in the physical. However, the law of grace enables us to achieve a higher level of consideration or come nearer to the beginning of this whole creative process. This process is a motivated movement from the spirit through the mind, which gives patterning of that force, into the physical, which gives manifestation to that pattern. As we work more deeply with our ideals, spirit and motivation, or as we introduce a high purpose in our use of the life force, then the purpose for which a pattern is awakened leads the expression of that pattern into a different form in manifestation.

We have built many patterns within the soul over many incarnations. These, like seeds, all have the potential for germinating and coming into fruition. But they can be energized by different purposes. If a pattern is energized by the purpose of helping others, it will manifest in one form. If the same pattern is energized by the purpose of self-aggrandizement, it will manifest in quite a different form. The same karma is met, but the outcome is different. Another way to view this process may be by using our old model of a cone or funnel to represent human consciousness in its relationship of the Infinite to the finite.

Thus the spirit, the force or energy, flows through a pattern in the mind (the karmic pattern), and brings a physical manifestation into being that conveys the qualities of the karmic pattern. However, when the spirit flowing through the individual is guided by a high ideal or purpose, the manifestation appears and is experienced by self and others in an entirely different form. While we can see how the karmic pattern is met, its manifestation is different because of the purpose for which it was mobilized. Thus, truly, we may change stumbling blocks into stepping-stones and we may see every experience which otherwise might be called karmic as an opportunity for the grace of God to work in our lives for the betterment of ourselves and others.

This leads us to a final consideration which is more important, more difficult and, indeed, more beautiful. Many who are oriented toward conventional teachings of the Church are fearful that the concepts of reincar-

nation and karma put aside or find irrelevant the atoning work of Jesus of Nazareth. On the other hand,
many who have been troubled by the doctrine of vicarious atonement find in the law of karma a more logical
and sensible explanation of how spiritual growth may
take place. Such persons feel liberated from a theological dogma which had offended them.

According to the readings, Jesus, by being fully obedient to the law, overcame the law and became the law.
God is law. God is love. Law is love. In Jesus this
reality was given full expression in the earth plane. By
virtue of this event, we have a new access to the Holy of
Holies and to the Throne. How so? We were made in
the image of God. The pattern of the Divine is imprinted
on our souls. Through the Consciousness brought to
us by the Christ we may have the mind of the Christ—
the awareness of our oneness with the Father. Against
all opposing forces, God established a thought form for
the whole world through which there may be a mediation between the Infinite and the finite—between God
and His children, who have cut themselves off from a
transforming awareness of Him. And in overcoming
the world and the law, He gained mastery over the
limitations of time and space so that He can be the
abiding companion of every individual who calls upon
Him, any time, and place.

Chapter Twelve

FREE WILL AND CHOICE

The concept of man's free will is perhaps one of the
most misused, misunderstood, and most debated. All
of us feel that we should be able to make our own
choices. Yet, all of us are too quick to blame others for
the circumstances or difficulties which we experience.
All religions are based on concepts of choice and respon-

sibility, yet many argue that God has complete knowledge of all that will ever be. If He is omniscient and omnipotent, then his foreknowing implies predetermination and predestination.

Any meaningful concept of responsibility, whether legal or moral, requires a concept of free choice, yet much of present-day thinking is based on a view of the nature of man that says all of our actions are determined by hereditary predispositions and environmental experiences. Psychologists and philosophers live and act as though they were capable of making choices, yet argue that such choice is logically impossible. Even those various teachings which maintain that man does have free will do not always articulate clearly the qualities of a being who would be capable of all that is implied by the term "free will."

A major reason for our failure to develop a meaningful concept of free will has been that we do not realize the implications such a concept has regarding the full spiritual nature of man as a soul. An adequate concept of free will requires an understanding that we preexisted in a perfect state and went astray of our own choice. Furthermore, an adequate concept of free will also requires a reexamination of our notions that a perfect God is omniscient with respect to our choices.

The Gift of Free Will

The information given on the nature of man in the Edgar Cayce readings provides us with an adequate basis for thinking through the functioning and implications of free will. These readings indicate that all souls were created perfect in the beginning as children of God to be companions and cocreators with Him. We were of the same substance as the Divine and thus also endowed with free will. For the will to be truly free, God Himself could not know what man would do with this free will. Else, why would it be said in Genesis (6:6) that God repented that He had made man. If God knew what our choices would be throughout eternity, and if what the omnipotent God thinks *is*, then how could it be argued other than that He had predetermined all the events in the history of mankind? Therefore, a major stumbling block in the concept of free will is the notion that a perfect God must have omniscience. This is an arbitrary and not necessarily logical view of the nature of the Divine. The Edgar Cayce readings put it this way:

> Having given free will, then—though being omnipotent and omnipresent—it is only when the soul that is a portion of God chooses that God knows the end thereof.
>
> 5749–14

This view of God makes for a living and open-ended universe instead of a machine-like and closed universe. We are capable of choices that are truly free because we are children of God, spiritual beings and as cocreators with Him, capable of truly creative expression which is neither wholly determined by previous choices nor by any other predetermining factors, including karmic tendencies.

In our understanding of free will, we must also consider universal laws. There is a lawfulness about the way in which things work. When choices are made which are not consistent with universal law, then the agent of choice—you or I—becomes relatively less free or more restricted than before. One universal law, for example, is "Like begets like." If a spiritual being, as a citizen of the universe, chooses to project itself into and function within the limitations of a certain dimension, then the experiences of that soul will, of necessity, be limited to the experience potential of that dimension.

To use an analogy from electronics, we as souls have all the senses or circuitries needed to tune in to any vibration of the universe. We are like an electronic device which could tune in on all TV stations, all radio stations, shortwave, longwave, CB, maritime, etc. But once we tune our system to a certain influence—as in selecting a specific TV channel—then it lawfully follows that we receive only that to which we are attuned. Thus, any desire leading to a choice which is less than the desire to be in attunement with and expressive of the Whole, will in some measure cut us off from an awareness of our oneness with Him.

There is another major problem in our understanding of the nature of free will which relates to our perception of the ever-present and loving nature of God. Let us say we may make a wrong choice. This choice may lead us through a series of difficulties to a new circumstance of greater understanding and joy. We may conclude, since the outcome is good, that it was not only necessary for us to go through the intermediate pain but also that we made the right choice in the long run. This continual working of God for our benefit makes it possible for us to change stumbling blocks into stepping-stones; but we should not let this obscure the simple fact that some choices are clearly better than others, i.e., some choices are wrong. By whose standards? By our *own* standards!

Even so, some who believe most strongly that man has free will, still try to argue that everything we experience is a part of God's plan and is needed by the soul to grow because "God is behind it all." Therefore, they erroneously reason that all is as it should be. Alas! Not so! Most of the pain we bring upon ourselves is not only undesirable, it is also unnecessary! It does serve to show us, however, that we have made a wrong choice with our free wills.

Let us now review some basic premises: (1) There is only one God, only one force, and that force has the qualities of being good and of being love; (2) we are, all of us, children of God, spiritual beings made in His image. From the beginning we were perfect, one with Him and had the gift of free will; (3) something went wrong.

The idea that *something went wrong* is often resisted, creating a stumbling block to a better understanding of the nature and condition of man. However, the only way we can truly reconcile God the Creator and individual responsibility for ourselves in our present plight is to understand that we went astray *of our own choice*; and by our own continuing choices, we put ourselves in greater disharmony or closer attunement with God and universal law. Since all is of God, then all is good; but the choices of man and what these choices bring into manifestation frequently are not good.

It may be said that fire is good because it is of the nature of God or spirit; however, if a man sets fire to his neighbor's house, this is not good. It may be true that the neighbor may experience some soul growth from this event, changing it from a stumbling block to a stepping-stone by the right attitude. However, it is not good for the choices of one man to impinge destructively on the lawful and creative expressions of another.

The victim in such a case may not be "innocent" in an ultimate sense. There may even have been a previous life experience in which he destroyed the home of another. The perpetrator of the fire could have chosen to stay out of the karmic web or the victim could have started the fire accidentally by himself. The victim need not have met his karma in the physical destruction of his home, had the choices, attunement, and right use of will of the individuals involved, been otherwise.

Choices

The concepts of universal law and "God's will" do not sit well with most of us who imagine that they imply a narrow, lifeless, and rigid design to the universe which would be quite limiting to us and no fun at all. Keep in mind that God is a Creator and His will is for us to give expression to creativity. He gave us free will so that we might be free and not like machines. God is truth and truth makes us free. God is love and His desire for us, beyond our greatest dreams, is for our good at the moment and throughout eternity. "God's will" does not imply choices which limit us through some strict, stern, and undiscernable moralism. "God's will" implies choices in harmony with universal law which give us greater freedom to create and express.

As depicted in the story of the Garden of Eden, a choice was placed before us: the whole of creation and the tree of life, or the tree of the knowledge of good and evil, the result of which is death. Unfortunately, we have always thought of death as meaning either the end of consciousness or the end of the physical body, rather than as a separating and alienating state of consciousness that cuts us off from a full awareness of our oneness with the Whole.

It should be very clear that whether we are speaking of the condition of our physical bodies, the quality of our relationship with others, or the attunement we have with God, that some choices make for limitation and others for enrichment. Some choices cut off the flow of the life forces and some enhance this flow.

Not only by virtue of the gift of free will itself but also throughout time, we are invited, "Choose ye this day." It has been God's intent and wish that we make choices. The concept of "God's will" does not imply that these choices are to conform to some fixed expectation on His part. Rather, they are for the purpose of experiencing the infinite richness, the varieties of life and love instead of the poverty of death and disharmony.

On occasion, people came to Edgar Cayce for vocational advice, expecting to be told of one specific job which they were supposed to do. Frequently, he would respond by saying, "Choose." To say that you are to do this, that, or the other thing would be as rote, and neither life nor God's will is fixed in any such narrow sense. It is true, to be sure, that some souls enter for a specific purpose. However, it is probable in most cases that such purposes could be fulfilled in any number of forms of expression.

Summary

One of the greatest of God's gifts to us, His spiritual children, is the gift of free will. It is His wish that we use this gift creatively and expressively. As we begin to make more choices based on the motive of love and in accord with universal law, we become less imprisoned, less limited, more joyful, more alive, more free, and more truly the companions of the creative God who invites us to be cocreators with Him.

PART FOUR
SELF-TRANS-
FORMATION

Chapter Thirteen

SPIRIT, MOTIVATION, AND IDEALS

In these times we are concerned about the motives of other nations and of our own nation; we are concerned about the motives of leaders, and would-be leaders, of special interest groups. In our relationship with others, we ask repeatedly: How do they really feel about me? Why are they acting this way? Are they truly doing that for the reasons they profess?

We are also concerned about our own motivations. We wish that we were more motivated to perform those activities which we value, and less motivated to perform those which get us into trouble. We wonder if we are doing things for the right reasons. So we ask ourselves, How can we change? How can we find it in ourselves to do better?

In the Edgar Cayce readings, we find unanticipated relationships between spirit, motives, and ideals. The spirit, the one force, is the origin of all motivation, and the setting of the ideal is an instrument for working with motivation. Let us consider in depth the nature of the spirit, motivation, and of ideals.

Spirit

The basic premise of the Edgar Cayce readings is the oneness of all force. For some, the word force seems to connote a neutral energy. Yet, another basic teaching of the readings offers a more complete understanding: "The spirit is the life, mind is the builder, the physical is the result." The expression, "The spirit is the life," refers to the spiritual nature of the one force as identical to life. Thus, when we speak of the one force as spirit, we are affirming that the essence of the universe is both intentional and purposeful, as well as active and alive.

When we say, "I believe in God," we are potentially expressing an insight into the essential quality of all Being—that there is only force and that force is essentially good. When we say, "God is love," we are affirming a further insight into the reality that the one force has not only the quality of goodness but also a purposeful direction of movement or activity which we can call love. By love we mean a mutually beneficial way to relate that has purpose, continuity, awareness, joy, and creative expression as attributes.

Now let us consider the teachings, "The spirit is the life, mind is the builder and the physical is the result." This may be represented by the following sequential process:

Purpose ————————→ Pattern ————————→ Projection
Spirit is the Life   Mind is the Builder   Physical is the Result

Purpose, a quality of spirit, provides energy and the motivational impetus. That energy, flowing through a *pattern* expressed, chosen or built by the mind, then manifests as a physical *projection.*

The Problem of Evil

As we establish the premise of the oneness of all force, we are immediately confronted with the contradiction posed by the apparent reality of evil. Our personal resolution of this problem is of the greatest importance because it affects our attitudes toward ourselves, our fellowman, and our relationship to the Divine.

There are three major viewpoints to be considered. One is the assumption of a good force and an evil force. Some of us are so intent on confronting evil directly as "the enemy," that we become preoccupied with a two-fold premise. Subconsciously, we become dualistic in our attitudes, even if not in our avowed philosophy. Thus, we place darkness in front of us instead of behind and become idolaters believing both in a good and an evil force. "Hear, O Israel; The Lord our God is one Lord." (Deuteronomy 6:4)

A second approach to the problem of evil is to assert that it does not exist. This line of thought may take two forms. One says the appearance of evil is only our misperception due to the lack of a higher consciousness. If we were better attuned, we would not "see" evil; we would see only good. The other form teaches that God's plan is one of evolution and that everything we experience as evil is simply the natural process of growth required for the evolution of our souls.

These two perspectives have great appeal for those seeking to manifest an affirmative attitude. However, they fail to address the essential problem of every soul: something went wrong and is still wrong within each of us, and it must be put aright!

A third viewpoint says that evil is real but is contained within the greater reality of God as the one force. For some, this presents a theoretical problem in the logic of evil as a subset of perfect Good, but, as we are told in Job 1:6, "The sons of God came to present themselves before the Lord, and Satan came also among them." It is helpful to think of evil as existing within God's permissive will while not expressive of His intentional will. The Edgar Cayce readings deal with the problem of evil in terms of this third viewpoint.

However, the real concern is not theoretical or theological, but personal. The personal problem involves first acknowledging that the evil with which we have to deal is within ourselves, then assuming responsibility for it. At the same time we need to develop and maintain a sense of the higher, more essential spiritual aspect of our being: "Ye are gods; and all of you are children of the most High." (Psalms 82:6)

We were all created in the beginning as perfect spiritual beings out of God's desire for companions to be cocreators with Him. As spiritual beings, we have access to the spirit, and minds with which to build from that source, and wills with which to choose how to build.

Evil becomes reality when we rebel and choose outside of the law of love. We went astray of our own choice, but a way has been prepared for our return.

This account of the nature of evil gives due recognition to its reality while neither overemphasizing it nor attributing it to a lack of awareness, nor seeing it as a natural accompaniment of the evolutionary process.

Now, the fundamental problem underlying the spirit of rebellion is one of motivation and of ideals. It is articulated by Lucifer in the Isaiah passage when he says again and again, "I will." (Isaiah 14:12–17) The fundamental solution, the spirit of obedience, is articulated by Jesus in the supreme trial in the garden of Gethsemane when he says, "Not my will but thine." (Luke 22:42)

God, having created us as spiritual beings with free wills, permits us to make choices which can project the one force into destructive and disharmonious manifestations. The reality of evil, however, does not lie in the nature of the force, nor in the manifestations of it, but rather in our own abuse of spirit, prideful motivation, and misguided choices. Any disharmonies which we experience are merely lawful consequences of the choices we make.

Motivation

When we think of motivation, we are more inclined to think of personal drive and self-interest than the drive and expression of the one force and our alignment with it. Especially in this time of assertiveness, individuality, rights, and freedoms, the concepts of obedience and "Not my will" give us serious problems.

We deceive ourselves when we think we can act independently from the purpose of the Whole without consequences. There is constant movement of the life force throughout the universe like the flow of a great river. We may be as fish who move in it, flow with it, and take life from it. Or we may be as rocks standing in its way. Sometimes by a crashing waterfall, sometimes drop by drop, the obstructing rocks are worn away, but the river flows onward. Can the will of man resist the rush of God's love forever? So, the problem of motivation is a matter of aligning ourselves with the flow of the life force—choosing life rather than death and allowing our lives to be guided by the current of creative force.

Physiology of Motivation

Within man are a number of qualities and motivations which may be related to the seven motivational (endocrine/spiritual) centers in the body. With this model, we may come to understand the entire symphony of human motivation as music played through seven instruments in their various combinations, relative strengths, and frequencies of expression.

Through these motivational-emotional centers, which we know as the endocrine glands, each motivational expression has its proper place. For example, we are physiologically constituted, programmed in a very complex way to be able to be angry. There is also within us, just as surely, a higher and more deeply seated Christ-pattern, encouraging us to respond in a fully loving manner. When our motivation is not in accord with the law of one, the law of love, then the activities and expressions of the motivational centers are out of harmony. The messages which these centers send to the rest of the body through hormonal secretions become contradictory, and the forces of the body are set to work against each other. Dis-ease becomes the inevitable result.

To understand motivation, we need to recognize the central roles played by the mind and will. It is within the ability of the mind, as the builder, with its imaginative and visualizing capabilities to dwell upon a motivational quality, thus selecting a pattern of expression or circuitry in the body through which the one force may flow.

The following is a commonplace example of the mind's

role in choosing motivational patterns. In a restaurant after a meal, everyone agrees that hunger has been satisfied. However, when the dessert cart appears, the imagination is captured by the array of tempting desserts. The appetite has been stimulated and a choice has to be made whether to order or not. Some may choose to remain attuned to the body's real needs, while others may allow the new stimulus to override the natural inclination. Thus, we see how motivation for the dessert is due to gratifying an arbitrary impulse rather than to the requirements of an intrinsic hunger drive.

Changing Motivations

If we are holding a singleness of purpose, then the one spirit of the life force may flow through us in unobstructed expressions of healing and creativity. As the mind, with its imaginative forces, begins to dwell more and more, as in meditation upon the pattern of love,' it becomes more and more surely the true motivation at both the conscious and unconscious levels.

The Edgar Cayce readings stress repeatedly that with application comes awareness. We often think we should not act in a loving manner unless we have a loving feeling; however, the reverse may be the more proper sequence. For example, a person may have a casual friend in the hospital. He may not feel like visiting the friend and may say, "I don't want to be hypocritical and pretend to care when I don't." Thus he may fail to go. On the other hand, knowing that it would be a commendable thing to do, he may bring himself to make the visit, and find it rewarding not only for the friend but also for himself. Afterwards, he may not only feel better about himself, but have a deeper sense of love for the friend. Thus, we may learn that in choosing to act in a loving manner, we may awaken the potential within to be more fully loving.

Ideals

Behind all of mankind's apparent problems is his spiritual dilemma. For any of our apparent problems to be resolved, there must be growth of the spiritual aspect of man. By "spiritual" here we mean "motivational" on the highest level. The spirit of rebellion leads to selfishness; the spirit of love leads to service to others and is the motivational basis by which selfishness may be overcome.

The setting of a spiritual ideal is a first major step toward reorienting the motivational thrust of the soul. An ideal is not a goal, It is a motivational standard by which to evaluate our goals and our reasons for pursuing those goals. The goal is *what*; the ideal is *why*! A spiritual ideal is not so much a goal toward which we move as it is the spirit in which we grow. It is a living and dynamic standard by which we quicken and measure our daily motivation.

Analogy of the MANTRA

Our understanding of the powerful way in which an ideal may work to transform us may be enhanced by a consideration of the true meaning of mantra. We have heard from the teachings of the East about the use of the mantra in meditation. However, no word is in and of itself a mantra. A word may be used mantrically or it may be used mechanically. A mantra, which is a mind tool, when truly used becomes mediator between the one force and its manifestation. (Remember mind is the builder!) A mantra calls reality into manifestation. It is like an invocation which, when uttered, is accompanied by the presence of that being invoked. We should use the word *mantric* rather than mantra, indicating that it is the spirit which releases the transforming energy rather than the word itself.

The setting of an ideal has similarities to the true function of a mantra in meditation. It awakens a high sense of purpose, thus opening the motivational cen-

ters through which spiritual energy may flow into manifestation in our own bodies and in our relationships
with others.

The word which we set as our spiritual ideal should
be one which, when dwelt upon by the mind—not the
intellect but the imaginative forces of the mind—elicits
a response in our bodies physically, mentally, and spiritually. Properly used, such a word invites and enhances
the flow of the life forces in and through our being.

When there is difficulty to be met, dwelling upon the
ideal enhances our ability to respond in the best possible manner. When there is discouragement, dwelling
upon the ideal enhances a deeper sense of the meaningfulness of life and the ever-present power and concern of a loving Father.

Setting the Ideal

At this moment, the step which you are being invited
to take may seem unclear, remote, or impractical. Yet
it is of utmost importance for each of us who have ears
to hear and eyes to see. It will allow the fullness of our
being to respond to this invitation from the universal
forces: "The most important experience of this or any
individual entity is to first know what is the ideal—
spiritually." (357–13)

Take a sheet of paper and draw three columns, label-
ling them "Spiritual," "Mental," and "Physical." Then,
studying the following instructions, record your ideal
under the proper column.

For the Spiritual Ideal:
What is thy spiritual concept of the ideal, whether it
be Jesus, Buddha, mind, material, God or whatever is
the word which indicates to self the ideals spiritual.

For the Mental Ideal:
Write the ideal mental attitude, as may arise from
concepts of the spiritual, relationship to self, to home,
to friends, to neighbors, to thy enemies, to things, to
conditions.

For the Physical Ideal:
What is the ideal material, then? Not of conditions, but what has brought, what does bring into manifestation the spiritual and mental ideals? What relationships does such bring to things, to individuals, to situations?

5091–3

After you have written your key word under "Spiritual Ideal," list several areas of concern under "Mental Ideal" such as self, home, friends, neighbors. Leave a space between each. Then with respect to each of these, ". . . write the ideal *mental attitude*, as may arise from concepts of the spiritual. . . ." What mental attitude toward myself should arise from the spiritual ideal which has been set? What mental attitude toward home should arise from the spiritual ideal? Under "Physical Ideal," with respect to each of the previous considerations of self, home, friends, and neighbors, enter an ideal *course of action.*

For further clarification of this procedure, study the following example. Let us consider a person who has set "love" as his spiritual ideal. When he comes to the mental ideal, he considers first, with respect to self, what ideal mental attitude should arise toward himself from this concept of a spiritual ideal. Then he may have a sense that to be more loving to himself, he must have an attitude of forgiveness of himself. He enters forgiveness as an ideal mental attitude toward self. Then under physical ideal, he may say, "To manifest an ideal of forgiveness toward myself, I intend to reestablish a friendship which I have neglected because of unkind words spoken." As he writes the letter to reestablish the relationship, he brings into manifestation (physical ideal) the attitude of forgiveness toward self (mental ideal) which grew out of the motive of love (spiritual ideal).

An Answer for the World

If you can bring yourself to take this step, to establish a spiritual ideal, you have made a major contribution to the solution of your own problems and to those of the world. The Edgar Cayce readings see this step for each individual as being of utmost importance. In a series of readings given on world affairs, a solution is given which is represented as being the only answer to the problems of man.

Man may not have the same idea. Man—all men—may have the same IDEAL. . . .

"Thou shalt love the Lord thy God with all thine heart, thy neighbor as thyself!" This is the whole law, this is the whole answer to the world, to each and every soul. That is the answer to the world conditions as they exist today.

How shall this be brought about? As each in their own respective sphere put into action that they know to be the fulfilling of that as has been from the beginning, so does the little leaven leaven the whole lump.

3976—8

Chapter Fourteen

SOUL DEVELOPMENT

Contemporary life has been characterized as a time of testing, and one of the major forms of this testing is in our setting of priorities. Choosing that which has priority is a special challenge to all of us when so many opportunities, activities, and relationships present themselves.

The Edgar Cayce readings state that *soul develop-*

ment should take precedence over all things. We have known this for thousands of years. Previously we were told:

> Seek ye first the kingdom of God, and his righteousness; and all these things shall be added unto you.
>
> Matthew 6:33

> What shall it profit a man, if he shall gain the whole world, and lose his own soul?
>
> Mark 8:36

But in order for us to set soul development as a first priority in our lives, we must truly, deeply, and firmly believe that the reality of our being is spiritual in nature. We must be convinced that spiritual considerations are indeed more important to us and all those with whom we have to deal, than other more seemingly real or tangible considerations.

One way to characterize the work on a soul development is by calling it *an affirmation that there is a greater Reality*, that there are higher purposes, and that there are more enduring truths than those which our day-to-day activities may seem to represent. The facts in support of there being a greater Reality are substantial, objective, scientific, and for most of us, verified by experiences in our own lives.

A Willing Spirit

However, even when we know there is a greater Reality, we lack the willingness to act upon these accepted truths by setting right and consistent priorities in our lives. Both the spirit and the flesh are weak, and we may let these higher spiritual priorities slip, convincing ourselves that the activities of the day are of greater importance. A ball game, a bridge party, a TV program, a new contract, an argument with a family member— these are given priority over a few minutes of quiet or a kind act for a friend.

Clearly a change is in order, a decisiveness is needed, a new clarity of purpose is required, a greater perspective on that which truly matters, is called for. In the days of ancient Israel, a prophet would periodically arise and proclaim to the people the need to change their lives. In the present time there are so many prophetic voices that speak in unconvincing ways to us, that again our ears have become dull of hearing. Yet, if we turn within, we hear our own still small voice entreating us. A change is in order!

A certain man came to Edgar Cayce many times, promising to live a better life. Yet, the readings frequently chided him because though he was often given good advice, he failed to act upon it in a consistent manner. And so, on one occasion, when he asked about the karmic relationship to his present development he was told:

> The body little understands the meaning of karma
> . . . Karma, is, then, that that has been in the past
> builded as indifference to that known to be right. . . .
> 257–78

In examining this answer we are reminded again that what is asked of any soul is simply to do what we know to do today. If we fail to act upon what we know to do, and build an indifference to what we know to be right, then we place ourselves in the position of meeting that which may be *experienced as pain and defined as karmic.* What is needed most, then, is a willingness, a spirit of willingness to do what we know we have to do. This same man was further told:

> Be willing to be led; not by spirits, but by the Spirit
> of God—Good—Right. Put into practice—day by day—
> that as is known. Not some great deed or act, or
> speech, but line upon line, precept upon precept, here
> a little, there a little.
>
> 257–78

Desire versus Will

Then what causes good and evil? What separates us from God? According to the readings it is "Desire!" Desire is the opposite of Will.

How are we to deal with these desires that are out of accord? It is in seeking and in choosing through the will that we seek first the kingdom and choose life! According to the readings no urge—physical, mental, or spiritual—surpasses the will of an individual. Provided that the will is made one with the ideal, there is no greater factor. No influence of heredity, environment or whatever, surpasses the will.

The Basic Pattern

Having set soul development as the highest priority in our lives, how are we to proceed? The answer we have from the readings encompasses a twofold procedure for soul development: attunement and application, or tuning in and pouring it out. The attunement comes in opening the self to the consciousness of the Christ-purpose or Christ consciousness. To achieve this we must invite His presence. This may be practiced in meditation. The application comes in "pouring it out" in spirit-imbued acts of helpfulness to others. The quality of these applications has been characterized as "the fruit of the Spirit."

This pattern of attunement and application is obviously a form of the great commandment to love God with all our heart, mind, and soul, and our neighbor as ourselves. Thus we may say that soul development relates most directly to the application of the great commandment with respect to our relationship to the Divine and our relationship to our fellowman.

As spiritual beings we have access through that spiritual part of ourselves, the soul, to be in attunement with the One Force, God, with Love Universal. As cocreators with him, we have the opportunity in the expression of this energy of love, to reach out in creative, helpful, and healing ways to our fellowman.

As souls, we were created by God out of his desire for companionship. Thus the desire to be in at-one-ment with Him in the fullness of the meaning of our love of God, is not only our own soul's deepest desire, but also the deepest desire of the Father himself. Our purpose as souls is to become companionable to that One Force; and compatibility is demonstrated through creative and expressive acts in accord with Love. Great deeds are not required. As a matter of fact, the readings indicate that in the material plane only little things count: patience, long-suffering, kindness, and brotherly love.

Personality versus Individuality

One barrier to the commitment to soul development that many of us face is the fear that putting ourselves in accord with *divine will* may lead to a loss of our own individuality. According to the readings, however:

> The more the entity applies self to those forces that are emanations from the spirit . . . (the) more individuality must be that as emanates whether in writing, drawing, painting or what not. . . . Personality is that seen by others. Individuality is that which shines out from within separating one from another. Though one may be but a dot, that dot remains ever individual . . . The nearer one becomes to that which will give its individuality, yet losing itself in the whole, the more individuality one attains!
>
> 345–2

We understand from the readings that the gift to us as souls from God the Father, was the gift of continuing individuality. Here we are instructed as to how this individuality may become most fully manifested: by attuning to those forces that emanate from the Creative Forces themselves, we can give expression to these forces in our daily lives. It is in this way that our own true individuality is developed and our soul quality manifested.

Awareness of the Oneness

As we continue to think of the great commandment as a pattern for soul development, let us consider the first aspect of this commandment: love of God. In the Scriptures we are invited to have the consciousness of Christ, who thought it not unseemly to be equal with God. This presents a complex problem for the mind of man. On the one hand, we fell because we wanted to be God apart from God. On the other hand, having fallen, we still cannot find it in ourselves to reclaim our divine origin and heritage, asserting that we are the children of God. We cannot find it within ourselves to have a consciousness of speaking with Him directly, face-to-face, like the prophets of old. The essence of the first commandment to love God, is to know of our direct relationship with Him.

The readings say that nothing should be more startling to every soul than that God speaks directly to his children. We are invited to meditate and this is defined as meeting God face-to-face on common ground. In one of the boldest statments in the readings we are told that God's greatest wish is that we would choose to be *equal* with Him. To insist upon unworthiness, is to insist upon maintaining a separation. It is a quality of the lower self, not the higher, that dominates such consciousness. But we cannot grow in the Godhead we deny. We cannot enter into a relationship if we insist upon maintaining a sense of unworthiness which is a denial of His love, mercy, and forgiveness, as well as a denial of His power to cleanse and to heal. The Christ consciousness to which we are invited is an awareness of the oneness of our soul with the Divine's. Our acceptance of this relationship and this love is made manifest by the way we act in relationship to our fellowman.

Now let us consider the second aspect of the great commandment: love of neighbor. We must see the Christ in our fellowman, even our enemies, and inasmuch as we extend our vision unto those who are the least in our own estimation, we do it unto Him. True love of neighbor requires seeing the Christ in others and denying, or rather crucifying, our own lower self.

In Patience

Patience has a very special relationship to soul development. We are told again and again, "In patience, possess ye your soul." (Luke 21:19) If patience is of such momentous import to the soul, then clearly we need to find it within ourselves to imbue this word with all the richness of content and spirit that it deserves.

What is patience? It is not a passive response but rather an active force. As literally an active force, it is the Spirit being raised within ourselves; this is best accomplished in the practice of meditation. If we do not meditate regularly we fail to raise that force which may be given expression in our lives in manifestations of patience.

In the readings, patience is even seen as one of the three dimensions in which we find ourselves in this present experience: Time, Space, and Patience. And thus, it is one of the ways in which God manifests Himself to us and in which we experience Him in this level of consciousness.

Patience also relates to the attitude that we hold about certain circumstances and the attitudes we manifest in our relationships with others. It relates to the quality of application that we manifest in all of our activities. Witness the following reading:

Oft has the entity found that so many disappointments appear in others. Know that first rule, a Law that is eternal: THE SEED SOWN MUST ONE DAY BE REAPED. Ye disappointed others. TODAY FROM THINE OWN DISAPPOINTMENTS YE MAY LEARN PATIENCE, THE MOST BEAUTIFUL OF ALL VIRTUES AND THE LEAST UNDERSTOOD! Remember, it is one of the phases or dimensions through which thy soul may catch the greatest and the more beautiful glimpse of the Creator. . . .

2448—2

Summary

Soul development should take precedence over all things. When we choose this as the highest priority in our lives, then we may see in the Law, the great commandment, a special pattern for soul development. This pattern, love of God and neighbor, may be conceptualized as *attunement* and *application*. These go together and are always inseparable. Attunement is best practiced in regular periods of meditation. Such meditation must have the quality of a genuine sense of approaching the Divine and inviting Him to enter into our lives. Application is best understood in terms of soul development, as a manifestation of the fruit of the spirit exemplified through the practice of patience with respect to ourselves and to our fellowman.

Taking these steps is not too difficult for us. They do not require more than we are capable of giving. All that is required is a willingness to do what we know to do; and in so doing, we bring immeasurable joy to our neighbor, to ourselves, and indeed to the Father as well.

Chapter Fifteen

ATTITUDES AND EMOTIONS

An attitude is literally a stance, a posture, an orientation. It is that point of view which we choose for the moment. Therefore, our attitudes reflect more directly the *nowness* of our being than any other quality. Our attitudes are also related to our consciousness; they are that stance which we choose to hold in consciousness with respect to all that we confront. An attitude, because it relates to the mind and will as well as the spirit, is one of the clearest, most immediate indications that man has a soul, a spiritual being.

If we endeavor to study the antecedents of our attitudes, and the ways in which attitudes may be changed, we find that the psychology of attitudes is extremely complex. Nevertheless, two or three things regarding attitudes are eminently clear. First, our attitudes are a matter of our own immediate choice. Second, attitudes clearly affect our behavior and subsequently the experiences that we undergo. And third, there can be no doubt that many of our decisions are based on attitudes held at the particular moment. With this in mind, it's easy to understand the effectiveness of TV commercials and the appeals of politicians, salesmen, and religious leaders.

If our attitudes are so much a matter of immediate choices at given moments, what is the relationship between them and the often far-reaching consequences of such choices? We may best understand this if we study the connection between attitudes and emotions.

Attitudes and Emotions

Whereas our attitudes are primarily a choice of the moment, our emotions are *reaction potentials stored deeply in the psychic mechanisms of our being.* These grow out of numerous previous life experiences and sojourns in the earth plane. How does the one affect the other? The choice of an attitude is like the selection of a *key* to a storehouse. What enables us, in making a momentary choice of a certain key, to enter into so profound a space within ourselves? It is the power of the imaginative forces of the mind. There is a very special way in which the *mind as builder* activates the response potentials of the body and opens the storehouses of karmic patterns. Thus an attitude dwelt upon by the mind turns the key in the lock to open the expression of deeply stored emotions.

The attitude or stance or point of view that we choose defines the nature of our relationship to ourselves, to others, and to the world about us. Here is the way it works. Almost any stimulus may become an occasion for a personal response. It may be an offhand comment of a friend, an item in the daily news, or the recall of an event in our past. Let's take one example. Say we hear an item of news about the world situation. Our initial response becomes a choice. We may experience this news as a call to prayer or as a personal threat. If we choose to respond with prayer, we may experience a greater sense of closeness to the Divine, a greater sense of personal worth and well-being and a reassurance about the future of the world. On the other hand, if we choose to view the item of news as a personal threat, we feel estranged, impotent, and pessimistic.

How does an attitude become an emotion? The major physiological response systems of the body are related to the endocrine glands and to the physiological action of their respective hormonal secretions. As the mind dwells upon an attitude it awakens appropriate responses in the emotional system of the body, the endocrine glands. These glands are known to students of the Edgar Cayce readings as the seven spiritual centers and as storehouses of karmic memories and patterns. We may think of them, for purposes of illustration, as collections of prerecorded tapes that have been accumulating throughout countless experiences during any and all of our incarnations.

When these storehouses are opened, whole complex potentials may begin to manifest in our lives. They may be seen in the development of a certain relationship with another person, the unfolding of a magnificent talent, or the course of a serious disease. These previously stored patterns and potentials are brought into manifestation in our conscious feelings and actions by the imaginative forces of the mind. As the mind dwells upon a certain attitude, the physiology of the body follows the representation in the mind. Then, the responses of the endocrine glands instruct the rest of the body in functioning, which is appropriate to the emotional patterns being awakened. The seven endocrine glands and their hormonal secretions orchestrate the responses of every cell, perhaps every atom, of the body. If the expressions of these patterns are out of harmony with the normal functioning of the physiological forces of the body, then disorder in our lives and disease in our bodies will inevitably follow.

Innumerable influences affect our attitudes, and these attitudes, in turn, often trigger our deepest emotional patterns. Thus we may find ourselves and our lives tossed about like corks on a stormy sea unless we have steadied ourselves and stabilized our responses to those influences. Many external influences may affect our attitudes; however, we may take charge of our own minds. In so doing we take charge of the emotions and our choices which affect ourselves and others about us so deeply.

Attitudes and Ideals

The following formula is frequently given in the readings: "The spirit is the life, mind is the builder, the physical is the result." The way we utilize this formula with respect to our attitudes is of central importance. In working with "the spirit of life" we are told that the most important experience for any entity is to know what is the ideal spiritually. Setting the ideal is establishing the spirit with which we intend to respond to all of life. The "mind is the builder" begins with the posture of stance or attitude. As we begin to establish the mental ideal, we are instructed to specify the attitude that is awakened within us by the spiritual ideal as that ideal relates to ourselves, others about us, and those with whom we have to deal. "The physical is the result," means the best way of achieving the mental attitude growing out of the spiritual ideal.

SPIRIT	MIND	BODY
the life	the builder	the result
setting the spirit	specifying the attitude	establishing the course of action

As we dwell upon the spiritual ideal, a foundation is built upon which we may develop constructive attitudes toward all phases of our lives. This in turn leads to applications consistent with these attitudes and the spiritual ideal. The mind as the builder is truly the creator of our bodies and our experiences, both here and hereafter. That upon which the mind dwells, we become both in body and in soul. Now with the choice of attitude settled, we cause the mind to work with all of its imaginative, creative, and mantric potentials. In response to this divine quality of the mind, the deepest physiological responses and potentials within the body may be called forth.

The attitude upon which we dwell becomes the mantra of the moment. The mantra, as a mind tool, is the way in which the key is turned to open the storehouses of all our previous emotional experience in the earth. Therefore, in a certain and very real sense, it is the attitude that we hold that turns the key either to open these as sources of karma or of grace. And it is of the utmost importance that we choose, in the *nowness* and the momentary focal point of consciousness, attitudes that are consistent with the highest ideal that we have set.

A Place to Stand

For the attitude to be constant in the face of all of the determinants and influences which would claim its focus, there must be established something within our lives which is stable and to which we may direct our consciousness. It is the setting of the ideal, therefore, that constitutes the construction of a stable place upon which to stand, a firm foundation for every subsequent attitude or viewpoint. The ultimate place to stand is in the fully established ideal of all that is most richly meant by a *belief and love of God.* When we say that we believe in God, we should not only be indicating an orientation of the intellect, but also affirming our deepest attitude toward the nature of reality. A belief in God should ultimately mean, then, that we are affirming good, that we know there is only one force at work in the universe, and that force is good. From this viewpoint we are always aware that the ultimate truth about us is that the force at work in all manifestations is itself ultimately moving toward that which is good.

The ideal of good, or God, or love of God as expressed in the great commandment to love God with all our heart, mind, and soul, and our neighbor as ourselves, is presented in the readings as the ultimate answer for all the problems of mankind. As an ideal the love of God establishes a singleness of intent and purpose as the motivating spirit of our lives. Here is a foundation upon which to stand with respect to our attitudes regarding ourselves and all other persons and conditions.

Ideals and Ideas

It is of the utmost importance that we learn in our very deepest response, the difference between ideas and ideals. We may not all have the same ideas, but we can and must have the same ideals. Often in failing to differentiate between these, we sometimes hear others expressing ideas different from our own, and we become anxious thinking that because the ideas are different therefore the ideals are different. And then, because another person does not agree with our idea, we suspect his ideals, his motives, his intent. Consequently, we may experience our best friends and coworkers, even our loved ones, as enemies.

One tragic form of this conflict is seen when individuals in a single family or members of various organizations have different religious ideas. When someone else dares to differ from us in ideas we may become so suspect of his ideals that we may attribute his efforts "to do good" as deceptions of the devil. This focusing on different ideas leads to polarization. On the other hand, focusing on ideals would enable us to see the Christ even in our enemies.

Choose Life

There are basically two postures or attitudes: we either face ourselves toward the light or we face ourselves away from the light. If we face toward the light, darkness and shadow fall behind. If we face away from the light, our shadows loom larger and larger. Life and death are set before us. We are invited to choose life. Life is attunement, atonement, at-one-ment. Death is a consciousness of separation. Light is the way of love; darkness, the way of doubt and fear.

Our attitude of the moment is the most immediate accessible expression of ourselves as spiritual beings. Here is the point at which spirt, mind, and will—the three attributes of the soul—come into an immediate focal point of expression. When the ideal is set and held, it quickens the spirit and predisposes it to right purposes. With the will we then choose that upon which the mind is to dwell in relationship to our ideals. As creator and builder, the mind now begins to awaken emotional responses within the body as well as behavior patterns towards others, bringing those qualities dwelt upon into manifestation, both in our bodies and in the environment about us.

Thus, the beginning point of creativity is, from its very earliest inception, an orientation towards life or death. And just as with the will we choose the attitude, the attitude we hold with respect to conditions set before us, affects our subsequent decisions. These decisions, in turn, are given manifestation through our actions and behavior as well as our relationships with others. Do these actions and behaviors we manifest bring us life or death?

Attitudes are not only held but maintained, not in a static but in a dynamic sense. The stability of attitudes grows out of ongoing postures or orientations we maintain toward ourselves and others. For example, one of the ways in which we may maintain an attitude is to collect grievances or grudges. We collect these with

respect to ourselves, other persons, situations, our gov-
ernment, the world. Then as we come to deal with a
situation, we find ourselves responding toward it in
terms of the grievances collected. Thus, a negative attitude is maintained. With the simple introduction of
another consideration, we may immediately generate a
new attitude. For example, we may for years have held
a grudge or grievance against a certain person; however, the minute we are willing to acknowledge the Divine
or to try to see the Christ in that person, the previously
held grievance may immediately drop away. Subsequently, we find ourselves in an attitude of grace
instead of karma with respect to that person or situation, and in turn our behavior toward him or that
situation is completely changed; it becomes alive and
creative.

Similarly, the Edgar Cayce readings indicate precise
physical effects attitudes have upon the body. For
example:

> To be sure attitudes oft influence the physical con-
> ditions of the body. No one can hate his neighbor
> and not have stomach and liver trouble. No one can
> be jealous and allow anger of same and not have upset
> digestion or heart disorder.
>
> 4021–1

Nearly eight thousand of the more than fourteen
thousand readings given by Edgar Cayce have been
referred to as the "physical" readings. However, it may
be more accurate to say that even these are physical-
mental-spiritual readings. For nearly all of these so-called
physical readings began with an invitation to the individual to change his attitude both about himself and
about life about him.

> All healing comes from the divine within, that is
> creative. Thus, if one would correct physical or mental
> disturbances, it is necessary to change the attitude

and to let the life forces become constructive and not destructive. Hate, malice, and jealousy only create poisons within the minds, souls, and bodies of people.

3312—1

There is much more to be obtained from the right mental attitude respecting circumstance of either physical, mental or spiritual than by the use of properties, things or conditions outside of self, unless these are in accord with the attitudes of the body.

5211—1

Do not consider so much what others should do for or to YOU, but what will you do for and towards others?

1889—1

Some of the most destructive of our attitudes relate to that type of self-concern that has its beginning in doubt and fear. According to the readings, fear is at the root of most of mankind's ills, whether it is fear of ourselves, or fear of what others think of us, or fear of how we will appear to others. According to the readings, the challenge and hope in dealing with this fear is:

. . . fill the mental, spiritual being, with that which wholly casts out fear; that is, as the love that is manifest in the world through Him who gave Himself the ransom for many. Such love, such faith, such understanding, casts out fear. Be ye not fearful; for that thou sowest, that thou must reap. Be more mindful of that sown!

5459—3

On the other hand, the readings indicate that the attitudes most to be sought are inspired and characterized by the expression, *fruit of the spirit.*

Remember—let every purpose, every desire, every hope be tempered with the spirit of truth; sowing only the seed of the spirit, love, kindness, patience. Those things bring into the experience not that of longfacedness, not those forces that would hinder from finding real joy. For remember, He is God of love, for He IS love. He is God of Joy, for He IS joy; a God of Happiness, for He IS happiness! And only those forces that are in the nature of fear and doubt, hate and jealousy and such, bring those influences that are destructive or disappointing in the experience.

2403–1

Let us, therefore, more deeply than ever affirm this attitude toward the Universe: that God is a God of LOVE, of JOY, of HAPPINESS. As we set our ideal *to make manifest our love of God and man,* we not only awaken the ultimate emotion but have the most stable place possible from which to view all of our experiences. If we view the Universe with this attitude, we will see the Universe smiling back.

Chapter Sixteen

DREAMS—
SCENES FROM THE SIXTH SENSE

According to the Edgar Cayce readings, all dreams *are given for the benefit of the individual, would (he) but interpret them correctly. . . .* (294–15). From the outset it should be stressed that it is the dreamer which is important and not the dream. Our notions about dreams must depend entirely upon our understanding of the nature of man, the dreamer: who and what are we as dreamers?

We have come to understand the usefulness of models in depicting the nature of man. One such model may be based on *consciousness*, the most essential dimension of human experience. We have the potential for both experiencing different levels of consciousness and for receiving input from different dimensions into our waking consciousness. Such a model may be depicted by a funnel; the tip of which represents our present, limited consciousness, and the open end, representing our access to the Infinite or to God.

Thus, we see that dreams may come from, or be influenced by, forces at levels which lie outside our ordinary waking consciousness. Another version of this model, which indicates the structure through which these levels of consciousness may interact, shows the relationships between conscious processes and the physical body, subconscious process and the mental body, and superconscious processes and the spiritual body.

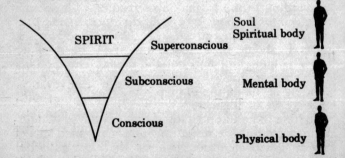

The main reason for our interest in dreams is due to the special access that we may have through them to the spirit within. One of the main problems of working with dreams is in dealing with unconscious processes, which stand between our waking consciousness and our immediate access to the Divine. Yet when depicted in our dreams, even these barriers become instructive.

When the magnitude of the vast realm of the unconscious is properly considered, the task of unravelling the meaning of innumerable dreams may seem overwhelming. But the great promise is, as the Edgar Cayce readings stress over and over again, that *there is not a question we can ask which cannot be answered from the depths of our inner being when the proper attunement is made.*

The Dimensions of Our Dreams

Many people wonder about the range of subject matter with which dreams may deal. For example, some people ask if dreams foretell the future. The answer, of course, depends on whether the questioner believes that the future can be foretold at all. Therefore, our understanding of the dimensions with which dreams may deal depends on our understanding of the dimensions of human experience. The Edgar Cayce readings portray the dream as dealing meaningfully with more dimensions of human experience than perhaps any other existing information.

We are physical, mental, and spiritual beings; therefore, the dream may be of a physical, mental, or spiritual nature. We are souls, and since "psychic is of the soul," the dream may deal with all manner of psychic manifestations. These include telepathy, clairvoyance, precognition, astral projection, communication with other dimensions including deceased friends and relatives, spirit guides, angels, the Christ, and even the voice of God. Every structure and process of the human body may be given visual or other sensory representation in dreams. Dreams may give invaluable information on the status of the body, including insights about what is helpful and harmful, as well as diagnostic treatment information for physical disorders.

All subconscious minds are in contact with one another. Through the subconscious, dreams may place us in attunement with those in the physical plane or those in the spiritual plane. We may be visited in the night by discarnate entities for many reasons: they may seek to give us assurance about their well-being in other planes of existence; they may come seeking our aid through prayer; they may come to bring us information which may be very helpful or limited; or they may come to influence us with their own desires or perspectives, which may be helpful or harmful. For example, there are dream reports of deceased relatives appearing and giving instructions about where to find a will or a lost object.

The events we experience in the third dimension are, as it were, a "past condition" because this dimension is simply a projection or a reflection of what is being built at another higher level. Therefore, when we tune into these higher levels, as we may in dreams, we become aware of what is being built, and what may be projected into the physical in the future. Nothing of importance happens to us that is not foreshadowed in our dreams! Which is not to say that all dreams are precognitive or that the exact detail of everything we experience is given earlier in dreams. However, the word "foreshadowed" suggests that we may glimpse and be warned of what we are building now which may come into manifestation later. We call these dreams "precognitive" or "prophetic" and when they deal with symptoms in the physical body, "prodromal."

Just as the angels spoke to men in dreams in the times of the Bible, so the readings say, "The Spirit of Forces as come from those on high, speak as often . . . as such forces did of old." (294—34) Some people came to Cayce with dreams of the Christ. None was told that it was simply his imagination, but all were assured they were indeed in touch with Him. A New York businessman of Jewish background dreamed he was being visited in his home by God Himself. He was dressed in a brown business suit and carrying a gray derby hat. As the dreamer showed Him about the house, they came to the owner's liquor cabinet. Almost embarrassed, he said. "In case of sickness," to which God replied, "You are well prepared!" When the dreamer asked Edgar Cayce about his experience, he was assured that he had indeed been in attunement with "The Whole Force, the Whole Unit, the Oneness." (900–231)

Because we have been incarnate in the earth many times, our souls within us carry the records of these past lives. Insofar as they are relevant to our present experiences or elicited by current stimuli, memories of these records may appear in our dreams in slight intimations or, on occasion, in extensive, vivid, and dramatic detail.

There is no dimension of human life, whether social, financial, emotional or physical, mental or spiritual with which the dream may not on occasion deal. Dreams may encourage or reprimand, instruct or deceive, inspire or seduce, guide or confuse. The potential for an immense array of experiences in consciousness is always there. What we actually receive depends upon our attitudes, motivations, the measure of our attunement, and the extent to which we have made applicable what was received in earlier dreams and in waking experiences.

Working with versus Interpreting Dreams

One of the great stumbling blocks to a more intensive and widespread use of dreams is the notion that dreams have a single right interpretation, which the dreamer has little chance of deciphering without highly skilled psychological or psychic help. The attitude that all of us can and must work with our dreams needs to replace the notion that only highly skilled people can properly interpret dreams.

It is erroneous to think that the dream has its origin

in some message couched in a "foreign" language of symbols, which in turn we must translate into our own language. The dream is a visual or sensory depiction of the forces that are being energized within our internal system in relationship to those other systems with which we are in attunement. The dream may be thought of as a report rather than a message. In computer language, it is a "read-out" of the internal processes which are ruling at the time.

Another thing which may be confusing is that the priorities set by our internal processes are not necessarily those we think of as important in our waking lives. As we recall our dreams, we may observe those things with which the inner life is concerned. The dreams may reflect the high priorities of the spiritual life or the detours we take, allowing our motivations to get us off the right track.

Whatever they may be, our dreams *are* what they *should be.* Therefore, we may truly say there are no bad dreams because the dream is an objective report on the complex combination of forces which are operative in our life at the time. We may have a bad reaction to a dream, allowing it to make us doubtful and anxious; or we may have a good reaction to it by discerning the need for correction and taking the needed steps. For example, if we have a dream about something disastrous happening to a loved one, we need not be fearful. The dream may be pointing up a need to change an attitude toward that person; meanwhile we may hold that person in a continuing prayer for protection.

When we dream of an undesired event, it may or may not come to pass. It may be a call to prayer which could change the direction of the circumstances, or it may be an advance indicator so that we can prepare ourselves emotionally and physically for whatever needs to be done before the event transpires. For example, a dream of the death of a loved one should lead us to prayers for guidance and for strength—for guidance if the event might be delayed, or for strength to accept His will. It may be the proper season for that person's death, in which case a dream might help us to reestablish a constructive contact and quickly complete any unfinished business with the person.

Working with dreams is a dynamic and constructive response to the whole potential of the dream, whereas *interpreting* dreams may become a static or passive response to a limited portion of that with which the dream deals. If we try to interpret a dream, we may ask, "What does this or that mean?" If we try to work with a dream, we may ask more broadly, "How is the dream instructive with respect to that aspect of my life?"

How to Work with Your Dreams

1. *Write down your ideals.* Remember the readings stress that the most important experience for any entity is to know what is the ideal spiritually. As we begin to make a record of our dreams, we should in the same notebook begin to record our progress with setting and revising our spiritual, mental, and physical ideals. If, for example, we have set a spiritual ideal to be more loving, and if we review that ideal in a deep and quickening manner before falling asleep, then we may examine the dream on the following day in terms of its relationship to the ideal.

2. *Have a seeking attitude.* If we have acknowledged and articulated certain problem areas in our lives and have determined within ourselves to be willing to take constructive steps in correcting these problems, we may more surely approach our dreams with the expectation of finding something relevant to these problems. We cannot expect to discern an answer if we do not know what the question is. Having posed some questions for our lives, we may examine our dreams for perspectives on these questions.

We should not anticipate or request dreams related to a specific question, because the whole point of dreams is that the conscious mind alone usually does not know what we need most. What is required is rather a seeking attitude and the willingness to work on every aspect of our lives. However, if we do make a list of some of our concerns, then we may in turn use this list both to help us recall our dreams and to sort through possible meanings of dreams. As soon as we become seekers, we put into action the universal law, "Seek and you shall find."

Some people advocate having the conscious mind program the subconscious for responses. But the whole point of the spiritual life is that the conscious does not always know best. Rather than the conscious mind telling the subconscious what to do, we should use the conscious to invite the superconscious to give what may be most helpful at the time. Even when we are viewing a specific problem and are in need of direction, rather than asking for a dream on that subject, we should mobilize a spirit of "Lord, be Thou the Guide. Thou knowest that of which I am in need." It may be truly said that the Spirit stands at the door and knocks. He will not be the uninvited guest; however, as we invite Him into our lives, we may anticipate a different quality of consciousness to be reflected in our dreams.

Thus, as we fall asleep, our preparation for dreaming should be a desire to affect the quality rather than the content of the dream. We know that suggestion can influence the content of the dream; however, even if a dream of specified content is received, it may be only from a subconscious response to the suggestion rather than a higher source of insight.

3. *Write the dream immediately.* Any serious work with dreams requires a willingness to record dream experiences on a regular basis. If only a single impression is recalled, a record should be made of that impression. Even the most vivid dream may be completely forgotten or later recalled in quite a different manner from the way in which it was originally recorded. The dream imagery is elusive and ephemeral, and it may be lost never to be reconstructed even within a few seconds of distraction. We may never begin to assess how many precognitive dreams we are having until we record

our dreams faithfully and review them regularly. A major process of working with dreams is moving information from the unconscious to the conscious. Just trying to record the dream even when all our words seem inadequate, is a great aid to the "consciousnessing" process.

4. *Consider the dream from different levels and approaches.* Having set an ideal, awakened a seeking attitude, and determined within ourselves a willingness to work on any aspect of our lives, we are now confronted with the recorded dream. At first it may seem meaningless; however, if we have recorded a dream which puzzles us, we may begin to ask, "Does this dream relate to my health, to my job, to my family?" As we ask and *listen within,* we may know intuitively to which areas of our lives the dream applies.

5. *Correlate those truths.* The readings indicate that the best method of interpreting dreams is to correlate the truths that are enacted before us. This requires a willingness to reflect upon the relationship of one part of the dream to another, even though they may at first seem unrelated. We must be willing to correlate images of the dreams of one night with those which we have experienced during previous nights; and we must begin to correlate the depictions in dreams with the knowledge and attitudes that we have from other sources—waking and intuitive—which are related to the imagery of dreams.

6. *Decide upon a course of action.* A full response for the dream requires a willingness to take a specific step as a constructive response to whatever understanding we may have of the dream at the time. As we do what we know to do, more will be given; and the more we act upon the measure of understanding that we presently have, the more surely we will be given more clearly an understanding of the next step to be taken.

This is the true interpretation of dreams—taking a step, however small it may be, toward a constructive ideal. It is only as we act on the limited measure of our understanding that we grow into a deeper and clearer understanding.

As we work with our dreams in this spirit, we may count on the promise indicated by the readings, ". . . happy may he be that is able to say they have been spoken to through the dream. . . ." (294—15)

Chapter Seventeen

MEDITATION

We cannot talk meaningfully about meditation without having an understanding of the meditator. To say that we are spiritual beings is to say that we are of the Divine. As such, we are not to seek Him outside ourselves but within, in the temple of our own bodies. The points of contact between the God without and the God within are in the body temple.

All healing comes from within; and there is no question we can ask which cannot be answered from within when we are in attunement. Yet, though we are children of God, we are separated from a full consciousness of Him. We are a mind cut off from the great Mind, a heart cut off from the Heart of the Universe. We are spiritual beings who have projected ourselves into a three-dimensional consciousness. Here, we have a physical body, a mental body, and a spiritual body. In ordinary life, whether waking or sleeping, the consciousnesses and activities of the physical and mental bodies monopolize our attention and keep us cut off from direct awareness of the spirit within.

With these concepts, we may now define meditation as attuning the physical body and the mental body to the spiritual by practicing silence. Meditation is reestablishing our at-one-ment with God and meeting Him within the temple of our body. The secret of secrets of meditation is realization of the godhead within us.

Seven Key Considerations

1. *Purpose of Meditation.* The purpose of meditation should never be "for" but rather "to." We do not meditate for something just as we do not love someone for something. The recent wave of interest in meditation encouraged the expectation that certain benefits would be enjoyed by the meditator. But the true spirit of meditation is more to express love than to receive recompense.

We should not meditate for benefits to be received, just as we should not love for benefits to be received. When we start listing the benefits that are to be accrued from loving, we move away from the language of love and toward the language of cause and effect, of karma. When we try to tell someone of our love, we do not convince him by listing the benefits we personally derive from the relationship. If we tell him we love him because he does certain things or because he has a certain quality, then he is going to ask, "Would you love me if I didn't have that particular quality?" The closest we can come to the spirit of love is to say, "I love you because you are you."

While it is true that highly desirable consequences will follow from the regular practice of meditation, if we have set out to achieve these things as goals of meditation, we have defeated ourselves from the outset. It is the *spirit* in which we approach the Divine within that is the key factor in meditation.

There is a story of a man who came to the Buddha saying he had been meditating for twenty years and was now able to levitate when crossing a river. The Buddha said, "You have been wasting your time; for just a penny, you could have taken the boat." The purpose of meditation is not to develop an ability, such as levitation; it is not to have an experience, nor is it to withdraw.

The purpose of meditation is related to the great commandment to love God with all our heart and mind and soul. In any love affair, we want to be near the loved one. "To love God with all our hearts" should be accompanied by a desire to be near Him.

If we cannot find fifteen minutes a day to awaken a feeling of our love for God, to express it directly to Him by seeking at-one-ment with Him, then we might well begin to question if we are approaching any understanding of the greatest commandment to all mankind. The working spirit of meditation is the spirit of love. We practice a period of silence in order to express our love for God.

As we eagerly respond to the first commandment to love God with all of our heart, we may be enabled in turn to better express the second commandment "To love our neighbors as ourselves." Psychic development, better health, an uplift of spirit—all will result from meditation; but the ultimate fruit of the spirit is love. Thus, love is the purpose as well as the outcome of meditation.

2. *Practice of Meditation.* Since there are so many techniques of meditation, we may rightfully wonder which is the right method for us personally. We may shop around, we may opt for easy methods or methods which produce certain results quickly. All are not the same; different ones produce different results. There are, to be sure, certain methods that are more sound, with respect to purposes and ideals, than others.

In any case, proper techniques should be followed. Some say the spine should be straight to facilitate the flow of the life force through the seven spiritual centers. The mind must be focused with a singleness of eye to focus the flow of the life force. The spirit must be quickened through desire with a high sense of purpose. Silence and stillness must be maintained. However, we cannot expect these techniques to guarantee results unless the heart, mind, and soul are centered devotedly on Him. Many expect that certain words will guarantee the presence of the God force. But no, it is not vain repetition but right spirit that invokes His presence, whether we use a mantra or the Lord's Prayer.

The most important thing about technique is our attitude toward it. Here is another Buddhist story, this one about breathing. How should we breathe in meditation? We can take a long slow inhalation, exhaling quickly. Or we can inhale quickly and then exhale slowly. Or we can inhale slowly and exhale slowly. When the Buddha was asked about this, he replied, "The important thing is that you breathe!" This answer lifts us above questions regarding the details of technique to a consideration of what is essential.

If the purpose of life is to become more loving, as we have been commanded, then the technique should relate to that purpose. If God is a loving spirit, we can attune to Him only by awakening a loving spirit within ourselves. We do not attune to the Spirit by virtue of technique, but rather in response to our own seeking spirit, the quality of our desire to love Him.

3. *Phenomenology.* We use the word "phenomenology" to refer to the personal individual experiences of meditation. It cannot be stressed too strongly that the criterion for effective or right meditation is the changed life.

There are, of course, experiences to be had in meditation and these are of a great variety. Basically, there are two kinds of meditation experience, good and bad, and it is difficult to say which is worse! Sometimes the "good" experience is followed by detrimental effects. There may be ego inflation; there may develop the misconception that meditation is to have an experience rather than to express our love of God; there may be subsequent disappointment if the same, equal, or better experiences do not follow. Seeking experiences builds barriers to their occurrence; and being unhappy about not having great meditation experiences is really fussing at God.

Let us take a brief look at the kinds of experiences people may have in meditation. Some feel dizzy; some feel a movement back and forth, a rocking motion. Others experience moving up and out of the body. Some people hear popping noises in their heads.

We are not deliberately seeking any of these sensations but, as the energy flows through patterns of thought we are holding that are not in attunement, we feel the effects. Some of them will feel undesirable and we may become frightened. Remember, the purpose of meditation is love through attunement. Instead of becoming preoccupied with or attached to these sensations we should refocus our attention, redirect our thought patterns to love for Him.

In everyone we meet and in every experience we have, we are offered an opportunity to meet God and we should not be afraid. Doubt, according to the Cayce readings, is one of the most serious and destructive things that happens to man. First comes doubt, then fear, and then destructive responses within the body. We do not come to meditation doubting the power of God to work in and through us.

As we turn within, we are likely to discover what it is that we hold as obstacles between ourselves and our awareness of oneness with God. When we try to be quiet, even for just a minute, observe where our consciousness goes. That is what our ideal really is, rather than God. What we think and worry about is what we hold in our minds and hearts in preference to an awareness of His Spirit. As soon as we become aware of our wandering thoughts, we need to acknowledge that these things separate us from Him, affirm that only with His help will things turn out right—or in the case of pleasant thoughts, thank Him for that experience—and then return heart, mind, and soul to loving Him.

We should never evaluate the effectiveness of our meditation by the experience we have in those minutes of silence. Meditation is not seeking a "high" in that period. It is rather practicing a regular invitation, day in and day out, for the Spirit of God to flow through us, transform us, and enable us to live more effectively and more lovingly.

The real transformation takes place at an unconscious level. So do not look too closely at each meditation experience. Do not expect to "see" or "feel" it happening.

4. *Physiology.* Because we inhabit physical bodies in a three-dimensional consciousness, there are physiological considerations in meditation. As stated earlier, we are seeking to attune our physical, mental, and spiritual bodies so that the spiritual purposes for our being here can be expressed. As a result, we must work in various ways to get the physical and mental in attunement. There are patterns within us that resist being raised and attuned. There are forces—whether they be foods, thoughts, emotions, desires, ambitions or whatever—which work against our attunement.

The Edgar Cayce readings suggest correlates in the flesh body to the physical, mental, and spiritual bodies. In the flesh body, the correlate to the spiritual body or soul is the endocrine system. The correlate in the flesh to the mental body is the autonomic or sympathetic nervous system. The correlate in the flesh to the physical body is the cerebrospinal or sensory motor system. The points of contact of the One Spirit with the individual lie in the endocrine system, which we know to be the emotional and motivational system.

The physiology of meditation involves all of these systems and is related to a hierarchical direction of the flow of energy from God into the earth through us. The reason we must be still and quiet is so that the sensory motor system related to our muscles and our senses will not rule the flow of the process. If our body is the primary focal point of consciousness, then that will work against any directing force which may come from within. If we can get the senses and the muscles to be quiet, then we can go deeper to the autonomic or mental level. There we still the thoughts, the heart beat, the respiratory rate. Then our purposes and ideals awaken the spiritual centers in the endocrine system.

The reason why we must be still is to establish first a contact with the spiritual level, then provide a direction for the flow of life energy to take. Also the direction of the flow must be from the spiritual centers (endocrine) through the mental (autonomic) into the physical (cerebrospinal); that is, from the Infinite to the finite.

5. *Preparation for Meditation*. Preparation for meditation should above all be on one's own terms and not what anyone else requires. We should not be discouraged or put off by asking, "Well, they said I have to do so and so, and I am not ready to do that—or I can't do this or that—so I cannot meditate." We must do what we require of ourselves in preparing for our meditation periods. The godhead we seek is a personal one, and meditation and our preparation for it are personal as well.

There are several levels of preparation which may be considered; and the following are offered as suggestions and guidelines. If we are seeking attunement, then preparation for meditation must be a continuing activity. We should begin some kind of gentle exercise. We should eat those things we know will help attune the physical body. We should feed ourselves a mental diet of positive thinking. Meditation does not stand alone. It exists within the context of our intentions to do something constructive about the overall pattern of our lives.

Some teach that if we begin meditating, the rest will follow. But Edgar Cayce said, Know where you are going before you start out! From the very outset, we must be willing to allow meditation to have an effect on our whole life. And we should be willing in all areas of life to cooperate with the meditation effort as part of an overall positive growth process.

Specifically, in our preparation for each meditative session, the readings recommend a prayer of protection just preceding the quiet time. An example of such a prayer is:

Father, as I open myself to the unseen forces surrounding the throne of grace and beauty and might, I throw about myself the protection found in the thought of the Christ.

6. *The Pattern and the Power.* In *Foundations of Tibetan Mysticism*, Lama Govinda has written about the principle of the pattern (which he calls "form") and the power (which he calls "spirit") saying: "Those that think that form is unimportant, will miss the spirit as well. Those who cling to form lose the very spirit which they try to preserve. Form *and* movement are the secret of life and the key to immortality."

In one of the Edgar Cayce readings the question was posed: "What is the difference between Jesus and the Christ?" The reading said, "Jesus is the pattern, the Christ is the power." What is it that mediates between man as a finite being and the Infinite? The power of the Spirit of Christ or Christ Spirit. Because we experience the dimensions of time and space, there appears to be a patterning to the flow, or a way that it manifests. That Way was exemplified by Jesus. As He perfected the patterning of His life through obedience, He grew to become the Christ, the Law of Love. That pattern He wrote in us, waiting to be awakened by our desire to be one with the power, the Spirit of Love.

The pattern is selected when we set an ideal. When we set love as an ideal and hold to that pattern, in meditation, then we have provided an optimum medium through which the Spirit may be expressed. The pattern within is selected and awakened and the power flows through it transforming our lives. But the power is not from ourselves, it flows through us. We must be aware of: "It is not I but the Father in me."

7. *The Promises of Meditation.* The Edgar Cayce readings invite us to take the promises of the Bible in a very literal way and to claim them as our own. The Psalmist acknowledged, "Though I make my bed in hell, thou art there." Jesus said, "I am with you always." The promise is that when we call Him, He is there. We need only to turn to, attune to, His presence. The readings also say that it is never too late, and that no matter how far astray we may have gone, we may always return.

Meditation provides a means for us to claim these promises. They come not for our own ability but through His love. As we grow in our practice of the silence, we may be given not only great energy and guidance but, more importantly, a profound sense of our personal relationship with the Divine.

Chapter Eighteen

PRAYER

As children of God gone astray, our most natural instinct is to pray. As we study the realm of the psychic and understand that psychic is of the soul, we may understand that the optimum, perhaps ultimate psychic expression, is given in prayer.

All psychic manifestations may be characterized in terms of three qualities: information, energy, and relationship. In the practice of prayer we optimize the potentials of all three. Information obtained psychically, rather than from the mind of another as in telepathy, is more optimally gained in the prayer for guidance. It is through such prayer that we receive information and instruction from the very Highest Source. Similarly, psychic energy, which can be manifested in psychokinesis or the psychic movement of physical objects, is more optimally manifested in expressions of healing. It is in healing that we may become channels through which the One Force may manifest helpfully and creatively in the lives of others. Thirdly, our psychic awareness of our relationships to others is most beautifully enhanced when we draw near to the One Spirit with prayers of invocation. It is especially true when we permit ourselves a sense of relationship with God, as our Father, and Jesus, as our elder brother, that we develop a sense of nearness to those whom we love and about whom we are concerned.

Some Problems

Although it is clear that psychic is of the soul and that prayer is the basic exercise of the soul, the importance and efficacy of prayer is often not readily understood. There are problems, primarily conceptual, regarding the role of prayer. One is the very appropriate question we might well ask: "Who am I to be telling God through prayer what to do? Isn't the only proper prayer, 'Thy will be done!' and doesn't God already know what is His proper will?" Prayer, however, is not telling God what to do but rather inviting the Spirit of God to flow through us, to someone in need, as an expression of love. The lesson for us as souls to learn is how to live together and love each other. We must learn to love both God and one another, and to use our access to the life force through prayer to give expression to such love.

Another problem for us in understanding the role of prayer, relates to the logic of understanding all human experience as being the lawful result or consequence of antecedent events, or as we sometimes say, karmic events; at the same time, we are obliged to continue understanding how prayer can make a difference without interfereing with the law. When asked about the advisability of prayer for another person whose problem was thought to be karmic, the Cayce source replied:

> When there are karmic conditions in the experience of an individual, that as designates those that have the Christ-like spirit is not only in praying for them, holding meditation for them, but aiding, helping, in every manner that the works of God may be manifest in their lives. . . .
>
> 281–4

Yes, there are laws; but this is a living universe and we are cocreators with God, and some things that have been set in motion, which we call karmic, are in need of change which we can bring about through the spirit of love.

Another very serious problem regarding prayer lies in our own sense of unworthiness. We find ourselves, or someone about whom we care, in need; but we also find ourselves seemingly cut off from attunement with the Divine. It may not feel right to call upon God when we are in trouble, when we have failed to seek Him when times were better. However, just the very sense of separation may be what the soul needs to bring it to turn about.

Another objection to prayer has simply been doubting the influence of a few words upon an extreme situation. As we understand better how prayer works, we may get a fuller sense of its potential.

Prayer and Meditation

The expression, "We pray in order to meditate and we meditate in order to pray," may be a highly instructive formula. It emphasizes the central role of meditation in making the attunement with the Infinite, which enables us to be channels through which the Spirit may flow in helpfulness to others. It designates the special manner in which this attunement may be enhanced by preparatory prayers, and how the Spirit once raised may be channeled to others in intercessory prayer. Also, it is this formula which enables us to make meaningful distinctions among the many types or forms of prayer.

First, let us examine the expression, "We pray in order to meditate." Many times as we would sit down to meditate and seek attunement of the physical and mental to the spiritual, we find that our consciousness is not fully directed; and our bodies and minds are not fully prepared to make the necessary attunement. Several kinds of prayer may be necessary to move us into the silence of meditation. Prayers of invocation in which we invite the spirit or the Christ to be present are important. They invite protection as we open ourselves so that the forces that surround us are those of helpfulness.

There must also be prayers of forgiveness, both for ourselves and others. Jesus taught us to say, "Forgive us our debts as we forgive our debtors." With each utterance of this prayer, we seem to be asking to be forgiven to the extent that we forgive others. To live in a state of forgiveness we must find it within ourselves to invite that spirit of love to flow through us even in relationship to those who have purposely wronged us. It follows that only insofar as we forgive others, may we live in the spirit of forgiveness and thus as it were, position ourselves as recipients of that spirit of forgiveness from the Divine that is always available to us.

Then there are prayers of joy and praise, thanksgiving and appreciation, which open the natural channels, through which the spirit of those attributes may flow.

Often when we meditate we are ineffective because we lack the full preparation which prayer provides. It may indeed be said that the preparatory prayers are a vital part of the meditation process. Meditation is seeking and permitting the attunement of the physical, mental, and the spiritual bodies with the Source. In meditation we quicken the ideals and purposes that stimulate the spiritual centers and their hierarchical ordering so that they become appropriate channels for the flow of the life force. To the extent that the attunement is made through preparatory prayer, the potential exists to direct the energy to others for whom we pray.

Now let us examine the expression, "We meditate in order to pray." This statement emphasizes the point that the only truly worthy purpose for meditation is the desire to be helpful to others and to serve as channels for the expression of love. If the meditation is for ourselves only, then we not only fail to make the full attunement, but we also fail to adequately disseminate and process the energy which has been raised.

How Does Prayer Work?

The instinct to pray is universal and does not belong to any particular sect or dogma, or only to those engaged in certain religious rite and ritual. All subconscious minds are in contact with one another; and with every thought we think about another, we are either sending helpful or harmful energies to that individual.

A way of defining man as a spiritual being is that we are focal points in the consciousness of God through which the one force may flow and be given expression. This expression may be at several levels: at the physical level in a loving or helpful act; at the mental level, in a constructive thought of prayer; and, at the spiritual level, in soul communion one with another. We may also be in contact with others through the mediation of other spiritual entities such as guides, or guardian angels, or through the ultimate Mediator, the Christ. The role of mediating influence is little understood and very, very underestimated in importance. The following diagram illustrates some of these points:

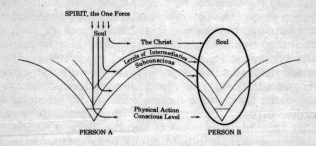

Let us imagine an envelope around the entity "B." Prayer directed to "B" may bring protection by surrounding the entity with light; prayer and meditation for "B" may, at his specific request, project energy right into his system. We must not seek to enter the "envelope" except upon the individual's specific request.

Even God does not do that. This differentiation between *prayer for* and *prayer and meditation for,* must be discussed in considerable detail.

The Edgar Cayce readings differentiate between prayer for, and prayer and meditation for, another. The essential difference is whether we seek to *surround* an individual with light, and invite the influences about that individual to relate to him in terms of this light; or, whether we seek to direct the energy raised *through* the individual as in a prayer for healing. Some people are dismayed by this distinction. They fear that they may not be as effective in prayer as they had sought to be, or that it indicates they may not pray for others except by request.

Now, to recapitulate: we may pray a prayer of protection for anyone and everyone, and there may be great help and efficacy in such a prayer. On the other hand, the prayer and meditation for another, such as in a prayer for healing, should only follow the request of that individual for such healing. For healing, there must be a oneness in purpose between the person praying and the one for whom the prayer is being offered. It should be very clear to all that if a person has a problem with emphysema as a consequence of his continued habit of smoking, the prayer for healing the emphysema without the smoker being willing to change his habits, would not be in full accord with that which is lawful. While our prayer of protection may indeed help the individual to be less vulnerable to advertisements and the smoking behavior of others, the choice to stop smoking must come from within the individual himself.

Prayers for changes contrary to the individual's desire may mobilize more of the spirit of rebellion within him and a subsequent intention to continue with the smoking habit. However, if the individual seeks prayer and says, "I want to be healed of the emphysema, and I want to change my smoking habits. Will you pray for me?" then another activity may be pursued which is called *prayer and meditation for* in the readings. Such a direction of spirit energy into the individual may indeed bring health and transformation.

As we continue to try to understand the way in which *prayer* for protection and *prayer and meditation for* healing may work, let us consider the analogy of a battery-operated radio. There are two types of energy which may operate in this instrument: radio waves and battery energy. The radio waves impinging on the antenna of the radio seem very weak in energy and may come from a considerable distance. The batteries within the radio provide the main source of energy which is modulated and patterned by the far weaker energy of the transmitted radio waves. As we send prayerful thoughts to another, it is not as though these thoughts must carry all the power needed for the healing!

There is within the individual a pattern for perfect functioning and there is also a source of energy from the spirit of life within. The basic law of spiritual healing is that all healing comes from the Spirit working within and through the individual. What our prayers may provide is a more coherent and higher signal. This signal may quicken within the individual the pattern of life and the desire to be whole. When this pattern is quickened by prayer and energized by the spirit flowing through the receiving individual, then the power flowing within is adequate for the healing that may follow. Thus, when someone desires to change and asks for our help, there may be no more effective way to work than through prayer and meditation.

To better understand the prayer for protection, let us pursue this analogy of the radio one step further. Perhaps you have been in an automobile where the radio picks up a number of stations. However, as you approach the broadcasting tower of a specific station, it may have drowned out all the other stations because of the immediacy and the power of its signal. In a similar way our prayers for protection may drown out those influences of a less constructive nature that would enter the system from without.

Let us take still another analogy: the mother whose

son goes off to war. She is concerned about two things. Will he be injured and will he behave himself? There is every reason for her to pray a prayer of protection that he may not be injured. As she continues to send him light, there may well be that presence about him that helps him step aside, so to speak, and avoid a bullet that he might otherwise have received. However, even though she is his mother, she has no business requiring him to behave according to her own standards or notions of proper behavior. Indeed, with such prayer, she may be trying to get inside his being without his invitation. This is not appropriate.

The prayer of protection for the son, in sending light, will be helpful to his behavior patterns by surrounding him with helpful influences. However, to seek to have him behave in the way that she would require, may not only be an intervention in the will of the soul, which God himself does not do, but may also be responded to, telepathically, with a negative spirit against those very standards.

This special emphasis on the differentiation between prayer for protection and prayer for healing should not detract from the variety of rich potential within the spirit of prayer. We can be thankful for others and send them our love—that, too, is prayer!

A Potential Beyond Limits

As we work with the principle of oneness, we who would be of help to others must try to do so at all three levels—the physical, the mental, and the spiritual. Because of our emphasis on application, we may tend to relate the practical only to the physical. However, prayer for another may be more helpful, more efficacious, and therefore a more practical expression of our access to the life force than even a physical act. Of course, our physical actions must bear witness to the spirit which we seek to express.

Yet, sometimes, it seems as if our prayers rise no higher than the ceiling. Why is this so? Although all subconscious minds are in contact with one another, this fact does not indicate the extent of the rapport that exists with another individual, or the level of awareness at which this contact is made. We may be in touch with another through our anger or resentment, our sexual desires and fantasies, our worry and fretfulness, or through the pattern within us of divine love.

If we select a pattern of love through which to pray and relate to another, then the Life Force of Love is drawn to us as a channel of that energy and flows to others. Becoming such a channel is dependent upon the extent of the attunement we make to the pattern of the divine within us, and our living with consistency and persistency up to the ideals and purposes we have set for ourselves. In short, are we physically, mentally, and spiritually in accord with the prayers being prayed?

We cannot offer that which we do not have. We cannot give love and forgiveness if we are not manifesting them in our own lives. We cannot awaken in another the spirit of purity if there has not been purity of expression in our own lives. We cannot quicken the spirit of the Christ within another if that pattern is not quickened within us.

If we will set the Christ as the ideal, quickening this pattern within ourselves in our meditations and let it be the standard which motivates us and by which we measure our choices and actions, then we may know the true potential of prayer, a potential without limits. It is then that prayer, like a tuning fork sharply struck, may cause responsive reverberations everywhere similar patterns exist.

How shall this be brought about? As they each in their own respective sphere put into action that they know to be the fulfilling of that as has been from the beginning, so does the little leaven leaven the whole lump.

3976—8

Chapter Nineteen

DECISIONS AND DECISION-MAKING

One of the most exciting and promising of all of the statements in the readings is the assurance that there is no question we can ask that cannot be answered from within. No matter how far astray we have gone, we may begin to attune ourselves through meditation and prayer to the indwelling spirit.

As we invite His spirit into our lives and begin to work with spiritual ideals, both to quicken the proper motivations within ourselves and to serve as standards of criteria by which to measure the motivational origins of our decisions, we may grow more and more in our assurance that the advice we seek can best be obtained from attunement to that spirit within us. The readings gave very specific and detailed information to many individuals on how to go about decision-making with confidence and assurance. Many people feel that their questions are either too insignificant or too important to be dealt with in such a way. Nevertheless, from the point of view of the readings, there is no question, however seemingly inconsequential or significant, which should not be approached in this way.

How to Obtain Guidance on Decisions

1. *Set the Ideal.* Here the ideal means the highest quality of motivation which the individual is willing to bring and by which he is willing to measure the decision. For example, a businessman may have an ideal of the selfless love of the Christ; however, he may have no intention of making business decisions according to such a standard. He might be willing to measure those decisions by an ideal of "fairness." It is better to set an

ideal with which we are willing to work than to set a higher one, having no intention of working with it in practical, everyday matters.

2. *Pose the question so that it may be answered "yes" or "no."* Apparently, the subconscious or the superconscious of the spirit prefers to respond directly to our decision rather than to give a discourse. If we are willing to work through the process of posing the question so that it may indeed be answered by a "yes" or "no," we may clarify not only the question but also the answer. The greater the clarity in the way we pose the question, the less ambiguous the answer we receive will be.

3. *Decide.* A choice must be made. At this point. we may bring to bear all of our reasoning, logic, good judgment and the implications of the facts as we understand them. Now we are to make our best logical decision.

4. *Measure the decision by the ideal.* Does the motivational origin of the decision we made measure up to the motivation which we hold as ideal in such circumstances? Sometimes the right decision may be made for the wrong reason! In the course of our decision-making process, we may receive a "no" to a decision because of the motive on which it was based rather than the desirability of the outcome.

5. *Meditate.* This meditation is not for purposes of solving the question but is rather a period of quiet for the purpose of attunement. At the end of the attunement period, the question may be reintroduced in a prayerful spirit, as in "Lord, I have decided to do this, yet Thou knowest best. Be Though the guide. Yes, or No? Then . . ."

6. *Listen!* We do not specifically listen for a voice, although that may indeed occur. We may have a visual experience, we may receive an affirmation or a proverb related to the decision, we may simply have a sense of rightness or a sense of being ill at ease about the decision we have made. Or, we may find one voice

saying "yes" and another saying "no," back and forth in an indecisive manner. We need not force the decision at this time. As we place it in the hands of God, we may later receive a clearer sense of direction through a dream, a new insight, or a new perspective. We must be cautious at this point about trying to read external signs instead of listening to the voice within. After all, the purpose of this approach is based on the assurance that we meet God within and that we can grow in our ability to sense His inner direction.

7. *Measure the decision against the ideal.* Once a sense of guidance is gained from the inner attunement, especially if the decision is changed, it must again be measured by the ideal. We are seeking a final decision which is consistent with our highest ideal and which is also based on a sense of inner attunement.

8. *Do it!* The readings warn that we must not make decisions in this manner and then fail to act on them.

9. *Be thankful.* The marvelous promise of a life guided by His spirit should be valued, cherished, and appreciated in the deepest sense.

Initially, it is recommended that this decision-making procedure be used repeatedly on low-effort, low-cost, and low-risk decisions. In this way we may clearly learn how the procedure works for us personally. This is a life process, not a single event. As we begin to make decisions in this manner and act upon them, we begin to grow in confidence, understanding the many factors involved in the procedure.

Soon it will be necessary for all of us to make sound and important life-changing decisions! The more quickly we set about working with this procedure, the more assured we may be, when more important decisions come along, that we have truly been guided by the God within.

The readings indicate that the decision-making process outlined above might take some time. We should not stop seeking help with just one attempt. The success of Step 6 (Listen!) depends, of course, on the measure of attunement we attain in Step 5 (Meditate). Occasionally we may be less centered or less attuned than at other times. But if the decision is correct, we should get the same answer. God will not be unhappy with our willingness to double or triple check Him!

PART FIVE
PERSONAL HEALTH

Chapter Twenty

HOLISTIC HEALING

Although the work of Edgar Cayce may be characterized in many different ways, perhaps the most important of these is that it was a work of healing. Today we
hear a great deal about holistic healing, yet decades
ago Edgar Cayce was providing information which contained an approach of holistic healing that is perhaps
still far in advance of other present-day approaches.

For Edgar Cayce, being healed, or being made whole,
did not merely mean becoming symptom-free or pain-
free, in ordinary terms. Rather, wholeness is a process
of at-one-ment, or becoming attuned wherein the physical and mental are one with the spiritual. The natural
state of our soul is to be one with God, one with the
Universe about us, one with our neighbors, and one
within ourselves. In these terms, none of us is presently whole and all of us are in need of healing. To be
whole we must be in accord with that for which we
were created.

As children of God we were created out of His desire
for companionship and for us to become cocreators
with Him. To be whole, we must show ourselves to be
companionable with Him. We must live dynamically as
channels for the flow of His Spirit, in creative expressions. Being well or being whole is not a passive state
but rather an active and dynamic process.

As physical, mental, and spiritual beings, we are
endowed with many modes of functioning. We cannot
think of ourselves as being whole unless we are actively
manifesting these functions. For example, there can be
no healthy blood vessel that is not carrying blood, no
healthy muscle that is not contracting, no healthy joint
that is not moving. We have legs for walking. How can we

have healthy legs if we do not walk? We are wondrously made for wondrous functioning. How can we be healthy if we are not giving expression to all these potentials?

If wholeness is living dynamically, in attunement with God, what is illness? The Edgar Cayce readings say that all illness comes from sin, whether we like it or not. To have a proper understanding of the depth of this analysis, we must revise our understanding of the nature of sin.

What is sin? We must put aside notions that sin is simply disobedience to an irrelevant moralism. There are laws, universal laws. By our free will and subsequent actions, we place ourselves in accord with or out of harmony with these laws. When we work out of harmony with the whole, this is sin. We build that disharmony into our own beings, physically, mentally, spiritually, and it manifests in illness. Healing begins when our desires, choices, and subsequent applications move in harmony with the Whole.

Integration and Timing

Holistic healing results from balanced, integrated, and properly timed physical, mental, and spiritual applications toward wholeness. It is not a simple multiplication of therapeutic modalities nor is it simply a wedding between conventional and unorthodox modes of treatment. Frequently, Cayce instructed people to make a certain application for a period of time, say, three weeks. After that step, and only upon its completion, a new application was to be introduced. These sequences, as given in the readings, should be studied for a holistic approach that includes a consideration of timing and sequence. It is not just a matter of so many treatments to be gotten over with—would you give a plant all the water it would ever need at one time?

Spiritual Healing

What may be involved in bringing together spiritual, mental, and physical approaches? First, let us consider

the spiritual. A spiritual approach to healing acknowl-
edges not only that God is the Source of all healing,
but also that all healing comes through the Spirit from
within our own inner being. Thus, healing is not the
result of merely external application or internal medi-
cation, but rather of attuning to the Spirit within. The
term *spiritual* implies a constellation of considerations,
including purpose, intent, desire, motivation, and ideals.

The purpose for which one wants to be healed is of
the utmost importance. Some, coming to Edgar Cayce,
asked if they would be healed. In turn, he asked why
they wanted to be healed—so that they could go back
to the same life style that led to the illness? As a matter
of fact, most of us want to be healed for just that
reason—so that we may return to our previous life
patterns. However, we may say that there are only two
good reasons why we should want to be healed. The
first is our desire to change—that is, change the patterns that led to the illness—and the second is our
desire to serve our God and others better.

Spiritual healing begins, then, as we reorient our
desires, purposes, and ideals toward being one with
and a channel for the flow of the Spirit.

In a discourse on the laws of spiritual healing, the
readings indicated that physical illness at its most basic
level may be characterized as the imbalance of the
rotary forces about the atoms of our bodies. If rotary
forces of the atoms are in balance, then there may be
healthy atoms, healthy molecules, healthy cells, healthy
tissues, healthy organs, and a healthy system. Healing
involves adding to or taking away from the forces about
the atoms, in order to bring them into proper balance.

The Role of the Endocrine System

The system most capable of bringing about the proper
balance of all the atoms in the body is the endocrine
system. When quickened, attuned, and aligned, and
working in accord one with another under the direction of the higher centers, especially the pituitary, these

glands may send out hormonal messages to all the cells of the body, awakening and instructing them in their proper functioning. In turn, the cells may be responsive to these instructions for healing in such a way as to affect all the molecules and atoms within each cell.

How is the energy of the living Spirit transformed into the three-dimensional manifestation that comprises our physical bodies? Apparently the transformation takes place at the subatomic level, within the atom, where the entering energy may bring the vibratory forces into proper balance. Here actual creation takes place. Furthermore, these special points of contact within the body, which are most sensitive to or responsive to the entry of spirit forces, are the glands of the endocrine system, which therefore may be termed spiritual centers, or sensors, attuned to energies of other dimensions.

How Spiritual Healing Works

There is within each of us a pattern, the Law written within, through which we may enter into the very presence of the Creative Forces within ourselves. This is the source of healing, whether healing for ourselves or others. When this pattern is raised in one seeking to be a channel for the healing of others, then that channel becomes like a magnet which may attune or raise the attunement of the one seeking healing. However, there must be oneness of purpose. The recipient must be truly seeking with a desire to be healed and to change.

When one who seeks healing has set a spiritual ideal and requested help from others, the sensitive centers in the body become receptive and responsive to the help that may be received. This may come from a distance, through prayer and meditation, or directly, as in the laying-on-of-hands. The channel is not the source of healing but one who may aid the seeker in attuning to the Spirit within himself. Prayer, especially when it is a loving and attuned response to one genuinely seeking to change and serve better, is a far greater contribution to healing than most of us ever imagine.

The laying-on-of-hands, which through the centuries has been fraught with much misunderstanding, is highly recommended by the readings. It need not necessarily be given by one who has the reputation of being a healer. But the laying-on-of-hands is not a momentary event out of which, if the recipient has enough faith, there may come instant healing. Rather, like other applications, it may be given for a length of time over a period of days, weeks, and months, to aid in the quickening and attuning process.

Mental Healing

Again as we consider mental healing, let us remember that there is a pattern within each of us to be whole and to function in a fully normal and healthy manner. In the same manner there is a pattern within every system of the body for the proper functioning of the cells of that system.

These patterns may be awakened and given direction for proper functioning through the directive, integrative, and motivational higher centers of the body. The patterns that reside within may be awakened by the imaginary forces of the mind. Therefore, for healing, there must be a mental diet that quickens helpful and uplifting responses, including becoming more deeply appreciative, the continuing forgiveness of others and ourselves, and employing a sense of humor.

Music, which may "span the space between the finite and the infinite" (2156–1) should become fully integrated into any truly holistic approach to healing. There is much to be rediscovered about the healing effects of music and the human voice.

The power of suggestion is strongly recognized by the readings and encouraged far more frequently than is often thought. The use of hypnosis and self-hypnosis to quicken and direct the healing process is occasionally recommended. In addition to a spiritually quickening mental diet, the readings would have us dwell upon the *ideal* with the imaginative forces of the mind in *meditation*. The forces which may be raised by deep meditation are the Creative Forces themselves. Thus, during the applications of physical aids to healing, we should see ourselves functioning in a more fully normal manner, and see the applications that we are receiving—whether a massage, a castor oil pack, or a glass of water—having the proper and desired effect.

Physical Healing

Now let us consider the physical applications for healing. These must be done consistently and persistently. Their purpose is to give the proper forces and incentives to the cells of the body for healthier functioning.

There are four essential considerations with respect to physical healing, and they may be characterized by the acronym "C.A.R.E."* Here we are referring to Circulation, Assimilation, Rest, and Elimination. Circulation includes exercise, massage, and adjustments. Assimilation concerns the belief that foods must be eaten in balanced combinations and with proper amounts of water. Rest includes setting aside enough time for recuperation, relaxation, and recreation. (The readings suggest that most people need about eight hours of sleep every night.) Eliminations include not only a dietary program but also specific applications of high colonics (a form of enema therapy), certain natural laxatives, steam baths, and other forms of hydrotherapy.

Special Roles of Osteopathy and Massage

The readings say that osteopathy should be the basis of all physical healing. The primary assumption of oste-

*The acronym "C.A.R.E." was coined by Dr. Harold J. Reilly, one of America's leading physiotherapists, who for over fifty years has made practical use of the data in the Edgar Cayce physical readings. Dr. Reilly is the author of THE EDGAR CAYCE HANDBOOK FOR HEALTH THROUGH DRUGLESS THERAPY.

opathy is that there is a pattern and force within the body for its normal functioning. Osteopathy is based not merely on adjusting the spine but also improving blood circulation. The theory is that blood carries the needed nutrients and oxygen to the cells and carries waste products and toxins away from them, so that the cells may function optimally. Let us add to this the vital role of hormones, which are carried in the blood as messengers to every cell in the body. Adjustments and manipulations are given to provide incentive for the circulation, as well as to remove any blockages, especially those impinging on the nerve forces. Osteopathy has thus tremendous potential importance in the readings because it's a technique for coordinating the nervous systems of the body.

With this philosophy we may better understand why exercise and massage are also special aids for healing. Massage is especially important in enhancing circulation in the lymphatic system, which functions to aid immunity from disease and purifying the blood. The lymphatic system has no pump of its own like the heart in the circulatory system; therefore, massage is of special value to this vital healing system. The application of oils to the body actually enhances the flow and the balancing of the life forces of the body.

Having grasped the role and importance of circulation, we may now appreciate more fully why proper assimilation is so important in providing nutrients to the cells of the body. We may also appreciate why rest is so necessary to permit those nutrients to be properly distributed and metabolized for the reconstruction and regeneration processes to be completed. Finally, from this philosophy it may be seen why proper elimination is so important. For the circulation of the blood to carry drosses and toxins away from the individual cells, the four eliminative systems—the colon, the kidneys, the skin, and the respiratory system—must be fully functioning.

A Definition

Holistic healing may now be defined as awakening the desire to be one with the Whole. In inviting the Spirit to flow through us in accord with a high ideal, or motivating purpose, we dwell upon that ideal with the imaginative forces of the mind; we give the body proper attitudinal and suggestive instructions; and we physically provide the opportunity for balancing the atoms of the body through the corrdination of the nervous systems and the proper circulation of the blood.

The Edgar Cayce readings are more concerned with thorough rather than quick healing. For one person, a complete cure was promised. When asked, "How much longer will this take?" the source replied, "If it's a day or a year, what's the difference if it's accomplished?" (281–5) One of the most frequently used expressions in all of the physical readings is that application must be made with "persistency and consistency." This is stressed so much that we may even say that it is in patience that we possess our souls. If there is no development of patience, there is no soul growth and therefore no true healing.

There is no condition that cannot be healed, provided we make our will one with the pattern of wholeness within. Certainly there is no lost opportunity for healing when we claim that promise that through Him we may be again one with the living Spirit.

Chapter Twenty-One

SEXUALITY
AND THE SPIRITUAL PATH

Before we examine the basic nature of sexuality, let us review once again our understanding of the nature of man. All of us were created in the beginning as souls, as spiritual beings. However, we moved away from our relationship with God through choices which were not in accord with Universal Law. As a wave of souls, we moved into the third dimension, the environs of the earth plane, and became interested in and absorbed by the evolutionary development there.

As this group of souls worked with the creative power of their minds, combinations of forms came into being, the origins of many mythological creatures such as the satyr, the mermaid, and the centaur. This first wave of souls became inextricably involved in these thought-form manifestations, and thus more seriously lost.

At this point another wave of souls, seeing their plight, came into the earth plane to help those who had forgotten their origin and heritage. With the entry of this second wave came the expression known as Adam and Eve, involving the development and new creation of bodies known today as *Homo sapiens*. The plan was to give entrapped souls an alternative and an optimum physical instrument in which to incarnate. Subsequently, they would begin to remember that as souls, as children of God, their proper natures were as spiritual beings, citizens of the universe, not physical beings incarnate in the earth plane. However, as the Bible says, "The sons of God saw the daughters of men that they were fair. . . ." (Genesis: 6:2) Thus we, of the second wave of souls, became involved with the first wave; we, too, began to forget what we were about and lost attunement with God.

Involvement in the earth plane meant taking on patterns of evolving animal forms, manifesting in sexual expressions. The development of Adam and Eve gave us an opportunity to do this in bodies that would also enable us to grow in an awareness of oneness with God. Remember, the first command: "Be fruitful, and multiply." (Genesis 1:28) However, even Adam and Eve with their newly created bodies stepped out of harmony with the specially prepared pattern. Thus we find ourselves as we are in the present.

The Spiritual Path

All of us, like the Prodigal Son, are spiritual beings who have come from the Father, have gone astray of our own choice and are on a journey of return. Each of us is a pilgrim on the spiritual path. We may follow the path by doing what we know to do and applying what we have learned, or we may get off the path with wrong choices.

Some philosophies teach that God is in His heaven and all is right with the world. They teach about a spiritual as well as a physical evolution in which everything is going just as it should go. We may make choices which seem to be wrong, but they are always right according to these philosophies. We need choice in order to experience something required for our growth, they say. Such teachings have very serious psychological and spiritual implications because they maintain that we make no wrong choices. It is deeply important to gain proper understanding of ourselves as spiritual beings with free wills, so that we may choose in *accord with* or *outside of* the law. It is God's love and forbearance that permits these choices to become growth experiences.

The perspective on the nature of man from the Bible and the readings suggests that we are astray of our own choice because of our rebelliousness. We must begin to mobilize our potential for being more fully loving, assume responsibility for the choices we make, and accept the consequences of these choices. We are invited, then, to set for ourselves a motivational criterion, a standard of purposes and desires by which we intend to measure our lives. Then, *in our own terms*, set ourselves on our *own* proper path.

Once we are on the path, then we may, especially with respect to sexual expression, suggest a map for discerning choice points on the path. Proceeding on the path, we are motivated by *desire*, a characteristic of God Himself who created us out of his *desire* for companionship, but we are advised in the readings to *normalize* our sexual expressions. We fall off the path when we go to extremes, becoming overly critical or self-indulgent. But we must still set our own spiritual ideal and begin to normalize, then spiritualize these desires in accordance with the ideal.

To spiritualize means to awaken within ourselves primary motivations that are oriented toward concern for the good of our fellowman, rather than for self-indulgence or self-aggrandizement. In doing this and setting a spiritual ideal, we clearly place ourselves on the spiritual path. In setting an ideal we establish a hierarchy in our motivational system in which sexual desires are placed under a higher motivation, for example, helpfulness to others.

To be on the spiritual path is to be a seeker. To be a seeker indicates that we do not have to justify our present thoughts or life style, but are rather willing to learn and encounter the possibility that we need to change. To be on the path means that we begin to guide our lives by the spirit within and not simply by rules or a feeling to reject or rebel against certain rules. The criterion given by the Master is, "By their fruits ye shall know them."

One of the special problems as we place ourselves on the spiritual path and seek to be guided by the spirit within, is that of a strict, self-condemning pathological conscience rather than a "still, small voice." Many who set out on the path become discouraged when they confuse this harsh voice with the voice of the spirit. *The true still, small voice is always forgiving and always encouraging.* The first step, then, is to set out our own spiritual ideal and to begin to measure decisions about our sexual life according to that ideal.

The Body is the Temple

The bodies, male and female, in which we are presently incarnate are products of a special creation of the

Divine Forces for awakening the consciousness of souls caught up in the earth plane. They were designed for two important purposes: to function as a system that would experience and survive in the earth plane; and to provide a place and an instrumentation through which the soul could become aware of its oneness with God. Both functions involve energy, motivation, and purpose. Therefore, the same centers or spiritual centers within us, represented by the seven endocrine glands functioning in the survival system, are also involved in the attunement system. In ordinary daily life, the system serving those motivations for sustenance, propagation of the species, self-preservation and self-gratification, tends to rule. As we seek attunement, the higher motives attempting to manifest love, light, and life begin to rule. In the integrated or attuned individual these seven motives function in proper relationship, one to another, with the higher motive of love as the guiding and ruling influence.

The body is the temple. We meet the Divine within our own inner being. The systematic spiritual practice which enables us to grow in this experience is meditation. Its physiology includes the attunement of this motivational or endocrine system. As we meditate, energy is raised from the sexual glands which make up the generative or motor system of the body. Energy flows through, attunes the other centers until it reaches the highest center, the pituitary, and overflows into the rest of the body, carrying the spiritually quickened secretion of this master gland. However, it is also possible that this energy, though quickened, may not be raised throughout the system and thus strengthen certain desires that could become destructive.

The motivational desires held by the mind's imaginative forces direct the energies in their flow throughout the system. Thus motives that are more self-oriented, express themselves in imbalanced and destructive ways; whereas motives that are oriented selflessly direct the energy and distribute it through the whole body in a

life-enhancing expression. Depending upon our highly
complex motivational system, sex may become either
destructive or helpful.

Mind Is the Builder

The readings tell us that the mind builds upon its
spiritual ideals or its material desires. In seeking a
better understanding of its role, let us consider the following sequences:

The Spirit is the Life	→ Mind is the Builder	→ The Physical is the Result
Motivation	→ Meditation	→ Manifestation
Purpose	→ Pattern	→ Projection

Mind is the mediator between spiritual energy and
physical manifestation. As we come to understand its
special role as mediator, we may more seriously reexamine the way in which we use the mind in thoughts
about sexuality.

We know that there is a kind of contact possible
between the minds of two individuals; we call it mental
telepathy. As we pray and meditate for an individual,
our thoughts impinge upon the other person with
respect to these motivational centers. There is a place
in normal sexual expression for mental activity and
fantasy. However, the individual on the spiritual path
may want to carefully reexamine how his thoughts
about sexuality are growing in his own mind and being
transmitted telepathically to another's motivational
system.

Usually we think of sexual motivation as primarily
physiological or biological. It is probably the case that
more sexual activity is motivated by the mind and the
desires upon which the mind dwells, than actual sexual need. It is the mind and its imaginative forces that
quicken physiological responses, which in turn are experienced as biological urges. When asked about the nature

and origin of desire, the readings said it came from the *will*. And those seeking were told to spiritualize their desires to help rather than to exploit others.

Sex and the Individual

When we think of sexuality, we are unlikely to truly reflect upon a relationship between two individuals. But thinking about the physical body and previous earth incarnations, we must consider the individual and all the sexual predispositions he brings to a relationship. The present influences, are not only inherited but also derived from experiences in other incarnations and other dimensions. According to the readings, our emotional life comes primarily from previous earth lives; the mental qualities come from experiences in other dimensions between incarnations.

The concept of reincarnation is an invaluable tool for helping us to understand the nature of our sexual impulses. In order to work with reincarnation, it is not at all necessary to know names, dates, and places. Reincarnation is most useful applied in general terms. The principle that there are no innocent victims, that we are meeting ourselves, is the foundation of a constructive attitude about any circumstance in which we find ourselves. Then, in writing our own karmic scenarios, we can develop instructive perspectives about what the previous life experience *might* have been in order to have set up the present life experience as a learning experience. Then our attitude begins to make of the experience a stepping-stone instead of a stumbling block. If we experience it only as a stumbling block, it may not only be karmic, but it may also persist. Meeting it does not mean erasing it. On the other hand, if we see it as an opportunity for soul growth, we may change not only the direction of the outcome in the present life, but also implications for the future lives of all concerned.

One of the expressions of sexuality with which our society is presently concerned is homosexuality. Several people came to Edgar Cayce with questions regarding homosexual tendencies. We may say that the Cayce source appeared to encourage and expect some to change their orientation. In at least one case, though, the source foresaw that the individual could not change. That person was told not to condemn self, that Jesus had never condemned, and that this circumstance must not be used by the soul as an excuse for not pursuing the manifestation of the spirit and its fruits in daily life. Also those who condemn homosexuality are setting up patterns to meet this impulse in a deeper, personal manner. Remember, judge not!

Another form of expression asked about in the readings concerned masturbation. On several occasions the expression *self-abuse* was used. This term may refer to abuse or overindulgence rather than being simply a euphemism for the word masturbation. In only one reading was the question posed directly. A woman of forty-four asked: "Is masturbation or self-abuse injurious?" And the answer: "Ever injurious, unless it is the activity that comes with the natural raising of the vibrations in system to meet the needs or the excess of those impulses in a body." (268–2) The term "unless" seems to suggest there are occasions in which the energy may be awakened so that self-release is a desirable, natural expression. Clearly the readings see masturbation as an alternative, if not optimum, form of expression.

It is always stated in the readings that self-condemnation may be as serious a problem for the soul as self-indulgence. The biological urge is present and it must be dealt with.

However, we are instructed to *spiritualize the desire.*

What is spiritualizing desire? Desire that the Lord may use thee as a channel of blessings to all whom ye may contact day by day; that there may come in thine experience whatever is necessary that thou be cleansed every whit. For, when the soul shines forth in thine daily walks, in thine conversation, in thine thoughts, in thine meditation, as it is in that realm where the spirit of truth and life may commune with same day by day, *then* indeed do ye spiritualize desire in earth.

262–65

Sexuality in Relationships

A frequently asked question within the readings regards the existence of soul mates. The readings' response is that the soul is the soul mate of the universal consciousness rather than of an individual entity. Therefore, even if there are souls who have worked together successfully in many lives, these should not necessarily seek each other out in the present experience.

The readings seem to see marriage as an optimum human structure. Some readings said that there was no need for anyone to be outside of marriage, if that was what they desired. In selecting a partner, the readings warned against a choice based simply on outward appearance or a physical attraction, for these would soon fade. Rather, the readings state, selection should be influenced by spiritual ideals, mental aspirations, and physical agreements.

Regarding the physical expression of sexuality, the readings state:

Do not look upon sex as merely a physical expression! There is a physical expression that is beauty within itself, if it is considered from that angle; but when the mental and the spiritual are guiding, then the outlet for beauty becomes a more *normal* expression of a *normal,* healthy body.

1436–1

. . . there should be *agreement* between those individuals in such relationships, and only when there is such should there be the relationships. For the lack of such agreement brings more discordant notes between individuals than any portion of relationships with the opposite sex.

4082–1

Decisions

The spiritual path is a path of decisions; the sexual life is a life of decisions. We are souls with free wills, invited to choose. As we establish our own sense of spiritual ideals, begin to awaken motivations appropriate to these ideals in our daily meditations, and to use these ideals as criteria by which to make decisions, we place ourselves on the spiritual path.

The psychology of the readings is unique insofar as it insists that each individual must compel or force himself to do what he knows to do or what he knows to be right. As we begin to make choices in accordance with our own ideals and inner guidance, we may be assured that there is a power greater than our own that will flow through us and transform us.

Chapter Twenty-Two

C.A.R.E.—
A POSITIVE APPROACH TO HEALTH

To be healthy is to be whole. We are spiritual, mental, and physical beings; and wholeness requires the integration of these three dimensions. To be whole spiritually, we must have a singleness of purpose set in a spiritual ideal. And we must be seeking to become attuned with and expressive of the Life Force. To be whole mentally we must have a mental diet that builds toward attunement and application, and we must consistently choose attitudes that are consistent with our ideals. To be whole physically we must allow the One Force of the Spirit to flow through us to build wholeness into the physical body.

There are many physical applications which can be made for developing and enhancing health. Most of us know but neglect using these applications which could, if applied consistently and persistently, bring into our lives far greater measures of health and energy than we ordinarily imagine. It behooves us, then, if we are seeking spiritual attunement, to take special care of the body so that incoordinations within do not cut us off from the flow of the Spirit.

The major consideration regarding health of the physical body may be summarized as *an attitude of caring.* If we *care,* then there is much that may be applied that will be of benefit.

For some on the spiritual path the care of the physical body may seem to be unnecessary or at best optional. For those who understand the oneness of the physical, mental, and spiritual, it may be seen that a healthy and properly attuned body is a very special instrument for making spiritual attunement. It is required of us all, then, to start exactly where we are with that measure of health we have, and to work with what is currently available to us. For remember, "He who is faithful over little will be given charge over much."

The word C.A.R.E. is a way of keeping in mind exactly what's involved in maintaining body health. C.A.R.E. refers, of course, to: Circulation, Assimilations, Relaxation, and Eliminations. A physical program that does not give proper consideration to each of these may be taxing on the body instead of beneficial. Let us consider these dimensions in order.

Circulation

There is within each of us a pattern for the perfect functioning of every system of our body. Healing comes from stimulating that perfect pattern in each system, giving it the chance to perform in the normal manner. However, there cannot be proper functioning if that system is not active. Therefore for optimum functioning, circulation must be enhanced.

The readings indicate that osteopathy should be the

basis of all physical healing. The essence of osteopathy revolves around the ability of the body to heal itself when proper circulation exists. If there are healthy cells, there will be healthy tissues and organs and thus, a healthy body. To have healthy cells there must be proper circulation. It is the circulation of the blood that carries the proper nutrients, oxygen, and water to the cells and carries away the toxins, residues or "drosses" as they are called in the readings. Thus, the purpose of osteopathy is to enhance circulation, both mechanically and by coordinating the nerve impulses to the various systems of the body. The beneficial effects of osteopathic or chiropractic adjustments, some of which may also be obtained with regular massage, should not be underestimated in the health program of an individual.

Exercise, of course, is the major way in which to assure proper circulation through all systems of the body. But many Americans confuse exercise with athletic conditioning. The Edgar Cayce readings, on the other hand, indicate that walking is the best exercise for most. If walking is not possible, then the alternative exercise recommended by the readings is swimming. Other exercise equivalents include adjustments, massage, and forms of hydrotherapy. Stretching exercises were recommended most—as in stretching the arms high overhead, and rising on toes when you inhale; then bending forward at the waist and moving the hands toward the toes when you exhale. This is to be performed as much as five minutes a day before an open window.

Another frequently recommended exercise is the head-and-neck exercise. Move the head forward three times, backward three times, to the left three times, to the right three times, then circle all the way around—three circles to the right, three to the left. This exercise performed five minutes each time, three times a day, may be very beneficial for the eyes and all of the sensory systems of the head. Let us examine this exercise in a little more detail.

We have suggested that the proper health of the cell may be maintained with proper circulation bringing nutrients to the cell and carrying toxins away. The head-and-neck exercise is a good illustration of how, through movement of the musculature of the neck, increased circulation may be brought to the whole area of the head. This provides improved health to all cells within the systems of the head. While head-and-neck exercise does not exercise the eyes directly, when there is enhanced circulation due to exercise nearby systems also may receive enhanced circulation and increased health as a result.

Assimilation

With our understanding of the necessity for each cell to receive its proper nutrients and to release toxins and drosses, we may reexamine the role of assimilation. This includes not only the intake of the proper nutrients and fluids, but also the stipulation that this intake facilitates the assimilative and digestive processes.

It is a simple and straightforward fact of biology that our attitudes and emotions affect the biochemistry of our bodily processes. It is also well known that positive and cheerful attitudes held during mealtime activate systems within the body that enhance proper assimilation of food, whereas anxieties impede proper assimilation. These considerations are not optional niceties, but rather simple lawful processes. We need not kid ourselves that we can properly assimilate our food if at the time we're angry or distressed.

Proper assimilation is enhanced by adequate intake of water, preferably a glass of water before the meal and a glass of water after. If the body does not seem to desire this kind of intake, then it may be developed by a gradual buildup.

The need for proper mastication of foods is another well-known fact which in practice is given little or inadequate consideration. The first experiment we conducted in our high school chemistry class was to test the sugar content of a soda cracker before and after mastication. When the fresh cracker is tested there is no indication of sugar. When it is chewed and tested again, sugar is present. The biological fact is that saliva is a necessary ingredient in converting unassimilable starches into assimilable sugars. This process can best take place through the mastication of the food in the mouth. If this step is not completed, it does *not* take place fully in the stomach or colon. This is just one of several important but often neglected processes, illustrating our lack of *caring* for proper assimilation of our food.

While there are many combinations of foods that are helpful, others should be avoided. We should tend to eliminate taking citrus juice and milk at the same meal, taking cream in our coffee, and taking wine with our meals. Citrus juice and milk may both be beneficial but they should not be taken together. Coffee taken properly is a food, but when it is old or stale or taken with cream, it is detrimental to the body. People suffering from constipation should be especially careful about excessive intake of coffee. Red wine when taken with dark bread in moderation may be beneficial, but contrary to popular notions about wine enhancing digestion, it should not be taken with the meal.

Pork should be avoided, save for occasional portions of crisp bacon. Less red meat, but more fish, fowl, and lamb will enhance bodily health. One meal a day, preferably lunch, should consist of fresh vegetables alone. Cooked vegetables may then be taken in the evening meal. Vitamins, of course, are necessary and best obtained in natural form through the proper selection of foods. If supplements are taken they should be taken *irregularly* and as a stimulus to the body to produce its own proper internal chemistry. Do not take vitamin supplements regularly and indefinitely, because the body may then lose its ability to produce those vitamins from the foods it ingests.

Normal body function is reflected in a litmus paper test of urine or saliva, showing a tendency toward the alkaline rather than the acid. This may be achieved by exercise and by eating foods that cause an alkaline reaction in the body. Carbonated drinks should rarely be taken, because carbonation itself is injurious to the kidneys. Fried foods should never be taken. The french fried potato is one of the least desirable foods imaginable.

All of these recommendations from the readings should be considered not as optional moralities but as lawful processes. You will see why more clearly if we use fried foods as an example. The readings indicate that there is an electrical activity functioning, almost as poles of a battery, between the liver and the kidneys. But the ingestion of fried foods interferes with the proper electrical balance between these natural poles within the body.

Two or three almonds a day may work against the tendency for cancer or tumor. An apple a day may not be all that beneficial because apples taken with other foods are not recommended unless they are cooked. If apples are taken, they should be taken alone. Tomatoes are an especially good food, but these should be vine-ripened. Unless vine–ripened, they are inclined to be more toxic than beneficial to the body.

Relaxation

For millions, perhaps most of us, a lifelong pattern from birth through our adult years is to resist going to sleep and to resist waking up. We neither have the proper attitude nor the proper evaluation of the importance of sleep. Sleep is clearly a universal requirement and the reported exceptions to it are so rare and dubious that it is improbable anyone can get along without regular sleep.

The Edgar Cayce readings indicate that seven-and-a-half to eight hours sleep is needed for most bodies. If you are one who says, "That's not true for me. I get along with six hours very well," you may be robbing yourself not only physically, but also mentally and spiritually, of some normal and important functions of life.

It is that which is needed for the physical body to recuperate, or to draw strength from the mental and spiritual powers or forces that are held as the ideals of the body.

2067–1

Two phases occur in the metabolic processes taking place in our bodies. The anabolic, which is the building up of tissues and cells, and the catabolic, which is the tearing down of tissues and cells. The building up process needs as much time and attention as the active tearing down processes. If we fail to provide time for this process to work in our systems, we may be contributing to an array of factors that may later cause disease and impaired functioning.

In recent decades research from sleep laboratories has demonstrated incontrovertibly not only the need to sleep but also the need to have a certain amount of *dreaming* sleep. Everyone dreams every night. If we sleep eight hours, about an hour-and-a-half is spent in dreaming sleep. It has been demonstrated that when deprived of this kind of sleep human beings, and other animals as well, become agitated and anxious. The periods of dreaming sleep appear cyclically during the night, about every ninety minutes. They become longer in duration as the night continues. Therefore, some of the longest dream periods appear just before awakening. If we miss the last forty-five minutes of sleep we may very well be cutting down our dreaming period by fifty percent.

We may be confident that dreaming involves not only the physical but also the mental, and spiritual bodies; and furthermore, that it is of great importance to all three. Even if we seem to get by with less than an optimum amount of sleep, we are cutting ourselves short on some mental and spiritual work that is vital to our overall well-being. Since dreams are occasionally sources of information, inspiration, guidance, creative insights, and spiritual experiences, the regular loss of dream time will contribute to the loss of some of these most valuable human experiences. Thus the quality of our overall lives may be reduced immeasurably by neglecting to avail ourselves optimally of this opportunity given in sleep.

In addition to assuring ourselves of the proper amount of sleep we also need to learn how to relax. It is a simple, useful, and easily learned skill. For one thing, learning how to relax may enable us, once we retire, to fall asleep more quickly. There are types of jobs and challenges placed upon all of us which could be met in far more effective ways if we practiced relaxation techniques at certain times during the day.

Three simple keys make for effective attempts at relaxation. First there must be a strong, positive, constructive mental pattern to counter that which may be stressful. For many this is an affirmation; others experience it as prayer. Some recite scripture or other valued literature that directs the thought processes toward enhancing life, joy, and confidence. Second, there needs to be breath control. This may be accomplished best by observing the breath and making it more regular. To this you may add the simple procedure of inhaling slowly, saying silently to yourself, "I am . . ." Only upon exhaling do you finish the sentence, adding the word, ". . . relaxed." And then third, relaxing by *visualizing* with the imaginative forces of the mind those various portions of the body that *are* becoming more and more relaxed.

If we have trouble falling asleep or if we awaken during the night and are unable to return to sleep, we should remember again and again this saying, "Why worry when you can pray?" and then use that as an affirmation to orient us to a consciousness of prayer, especially prayers of thanksgiving and prayers for others in need. We will find, then, that the time awake will be very well spent, and also that there will be a reduction of anxiety, both about those things that worry us and about the loss of sleep itself. By this practice we may find that prayer is indeed very soporific.

As an aid to falling asleep, gentle exercise for the

large muscles of the lower body, a glass of warm milk with a teaspoon of honey, reading of something inspirational, and active prayer and meditation are always beneficial.

Dr. Harold J. Reilly, one of America's leading physiotherapists, maintains that one hour of massage is worth four hours of normal sleep or other rest. If we find ourselves running a sleep debt, we might do very well to utilize this marvelous healing modality of the full body massage. On one occasion Edgar Cayce said that five to seven minutes of meditation immediately upon awakening might be worth several hours of normal rest.

Eliminations

Proper eliminations are vital to the health of every organ, tissue and cell in the body, and yet little attention is given to this extremely important process. There are, as we all know, four systems of the body that participate in the overall eliminative processes: the lungs, the skin, the kidneys, and the bowels. For the lungs to function properly there must be some form of exercise vigorous enough to cause deep breathing on a regular basis. Smoking, if engaged in, must be moderate. Posture should be given considerable attention. It is well known that the muscles involved in proper posture in the human body are not naturally maintained in proper tonicity. Proper posture requires attention and habitual practice.

The skin, of course, as part of the eliminative system, should be cared for as any other system, not just for cosmetic purposes, but for reasons of general health. There should be the periodic whole body massage with oils such as peanut oil, olive oil or a specially designed oil from the Edgar Cayce readings such as:

To six ounces of peanut oil, add: Olive oil . . . two ounces, Rose Water . . . two ounces, Lanolin, dissolved . . . one tablespoonful.

1968–7

For care of the skin the readings recommend a pure Castile soap for most. Deodorants must not be of the anti-perspirant type that close the pores of the skin.

Proper functioning of the kidneys requires six to eight glasses of water a day, and the elimination of certain foods such as carbonated drinks and large quantities of alcohol.

Proper care of the colon involves three major processes. First, proper diet including raw vegetables that give the necessary roughage; second, proper and appropriate cleansing of the colon, meaning, on occasion, a mild laxative, colonic, or enema. These are never to be depended upon as a regular part of the routine, nor should we eliminate them completely. As a matter of fact the bowels should never go through a twenty-four hour period without elimination. The scientifically administered high colonic is highly recommended in the readings as a periodic part of our health care. The home administered enema, carefully and properly given, may be very valuable. This enema may include two sequences: the first with a teaspoon of salt and a teaspoon of soda for each quart of water to keep the toxins from being reabsorbed; the second with a tablespoon of Glycothymoline for each quart of water to enhance the cleansing of the colon. The third major consideration is the willingness on our part to take the necessary amount of time, giving due attention to the proper elimination of the bowel.

Osteopathic adjustments, exercise, dietary considerations—all make a contribution to proper elimination.

Conclusion

Part of the consciousness of the new age is that every individual must not only assume responsibility for his own health but should embrace such an opportunity in a joyous manner—as an act of thanksgiving for experiencing these bodies which are the temple of the living God. There is excellent information available not only through several publications based on the Edgar

Cayce readings but also through other sources that make it unnecessary for anyone to be ignorant of a proper and holistic approach to the care of their own health. *CARE* is the key word, and by *caring* deeply within ourselves, we will find this C.A.R.E. formula an excellent basis for a positive approach to health and to a more helpful, creative, and joyous life.

Chapter Twenty-Three

REJUVENATION

The Fountain of Youth has been a quest of mankind throughout the ages. Ponce de Leon has been immortalized, if not for finding the wondrous waters which he sought exploring Florida, then in the history texts of generations of schoolchildren who read about his quest. The idea of a Fountain of Youth, however, is more than just a vain longing for rejuvenation and longevity; rather, it represents an archetypal pattern hidden deep within our own unconscious, which yields to us intimations of the possibility of the continuity of life.

As we explore the Edgar Cayce readings, we find that the goal of this quest lies within our own selves. In the readings we find some amazing statements regarding the possibilities of rejuvenation, as well as instructions for bringing about such regenerative processes.

> Keep the pineal gland operating and you won't grow old—you will always be young.
>
> 294–141

> ... would the assimilations and eliminations be kept near normal in the human family, the days might be extended to whatever period as was so desired.
>
> 311–4

How are we to understand all that may be required of us in seeking this Fountain of Youth in the waters that may spring up from within our own inner being? We find a key in the expression or concept of holistic healing. Remember, "holistic healing" contains a redundancy—because true healing means being made whole. But the expression "holistic" implies the special relationship among the physical, the mental, and the spiritual. To find the Fountain of Youth, as it were, is to meet the conditions required in all of these dimensions of our being and in integrated relationships, one with another.

Let us first consider the spiritual. We have been told that the great commandment is to love God with all our heart, mind, and soul. What does it mean to love God? God is Love. God is Life. To love God is to love Life. And to love life is to love that which enhances life, in ourselves and in the lives of others. To love that which enhances life in ourselves is to love those qualities of spirit, mind, and body which enhance life.

Do we love to eat the proper foods, to obtain the proper rest, to engage in the proper amount of activity? Do we love to have the mind directed and fed upon that which is uplifting of body and spirit? Do we love to engage in activities which bring life, light, and love to all of those about us?

In their invitation to all of us to follow the great commandment, the Edgar Cayce readings encourage us to be on fire with our love for the Infinite. Do we love the universality and the all-encompassing inclusiveness of the Infinite? And do we love the promise of "many mansions" beyond our life on this earth plane? Do we love to have the Spirit enter into, guide, and direct our own lives? Do we love to take the time to be still and quiet enough to attain the attunement through which the Spiritual forces may enter? Do we love our fellowman? Do we love him enough that we would lay down our life, or live our life for him?

Regarding love for others, it is interesting to reflect on those few individuals told by Cayce that it would not be necessary to return incarnate in this plane. What were their special qualities? Repeatedly, these individuals were told that they had loved, loved, loved, given, given, given, served, served, served—in selfless and self-sacrificing ways. Do we love the prospect of a life dedicated to the service of others?

The Edgar Cayce readings say that the most important experience for any entity is to know what is the ideal spiritually. This means that we are to set high motivational standards for ourselves, to try to awaken these highest motives in our every thought and deed, and to measure our decisions and judgments by these high purposes. Do we love the idea of setting about establishing for ourselves a high sense of ideals and purposes, measuring our lives, our thoughts, our attitudes, and our decisions by these standards?

At the mental level, we are told that Mind is the Builder. Here we are not referring to the intellect, but rather to that quality of the mind that is seen in the imaginative forces, relating not only to the conscious but to the subconscious and superconscious as well. The role of the mind as builder can be understood as we observe within ourselves the effect upon our lives of that upon which we dwell mentally.

As we contemplate more and more the prospect of a chocolate ice cream dessert awaiting us in the refrigerator just a room away, we are likely to experience a growing appetite we find difficult to deny. Should this become a regular practice, the consequence of the mind as builder in this case, may be readily observed upon the bathroom scales!

But the concept of the mind as presented in the Edgar Cayce readings is far more rich, profound, and complex than any we may have otherwise come across. The mind in the sense of imaginative forces, as referred to in the readings, is associated specifically with the hormonal activities of the pineal gland. To keep the pineal gland operating is to keep the imaginative forces operating. Just as the macrocosmic Christ is the builder, as the Logos in the Christian Trinity, so the microcosmic mind is the builder in the trinity of the body, mind, and spirit within ourselves.

The mind, and its physiological correlate in the pineal gland, is especially associated with the autonomic nervous system and with the subconscious mind. In this context, we may understand that the expression "mind is the builder" relates not only to the imaginative forces of the conscious mind, but also to the amenability to suggestion of the subconscious mind. Thus, all that we feed ourselves by way of suggestions, subliminally or in terms of what we say or think about ourselves, has an effect upon the functioning of the mind, on the subconscious, and on the autonomic nervous system.

The mind, in its relationship to the pineal, and the pineal gland in its special relationship to another gland, the Cells of Leydig, bear a special relationship to that process which may be awakened in deep meditation; it is known as the raising of the Kundalini forces within the spiritual centers of the body.

The raising of the Kundalini forces throughout the endocrine glands of the body, culminates in a quickening of the pituitary, which responds by sending directive and integrating hormones to all the cells of the body. All of this plays an essential role in the process of rejuvenation.

We now have a physiological site and process by which to understand the true basis for the indwelling archetypal pattern upon which the quest for the Fountain of Youth is based. It is the Cells of Leydig, the second of the spiritual centers in the body, corresponding to the element of water, which is the quickening point for the Kundalini. In deep meditation, the Kundalini is raised, bringing higher consciousness, healing, and rejuvenation; and it is the mind dwelling upon the ideal that is the key to raising the Kundalini.

The special relationship between the mind and the spirit is that it is out of an obedient spirit that we may choose the proper ideal; and, it is with the mind that we may dwell upon that ideal to build the highest motivational forces within the physical, mental, and spiritual structures within ourselves.

Physically, the process of regeneration is based on several concepts, which according to the Cayce readings have a solid scientific basis. These readings indicate that all healing comes from within, and that the body has within itself a pattern for its perfect functioning. The basis of the processes of the physical body may be viewed more in terms of physics than biology. The basic unit of the body is the atomic structure, and there are rotary forces about the atom which may become unbalanced.

According to the readings, physical healing is based upon the proper balancing of the rotary forces of the atom. When brought into proper balance, we have healthy atoms, and therefore healthy molecules, healthy cells, healthy tissues, healthy organs, and a healthy, integrated physical system.

Furthermore, the readings indicate that the body's inclination is to renew itself! Each organ has a cycle of renewal, the overall outcome of which is that the whole body is entirely renewed in every seven-year cycle. Thus, if any disease is treated consistently and persistently, it may be thoroughly healed if the seven-year cycle is observed and the applications are given throughout the period.

Now let us review briefly the consideration mentioned at the beginning of this chapter: maintaining the proper assimilations and eliminations. The intake of proper foods in the proper manner, and in the proper combinations, together with attention to the several processes involved in proper eliminations, are the key to extending the life span. Part of our "paying the price" for this goal is a willingness to adjust our diets and our lifestyles, enabling us to ingest only that which has the promise of being life-enhancing and to be sure to take the time and make the effort to keep the body clean through the proper eliminative processes.

Ours is a time in which we are learning why we age, and what we may do to slow the process. In addition to the information in the Edgar Cayce readings, there are a number of insights from other sources which we may apply in our quest for continuing health.

However, the biggest question remains in this soul-searching query of the readings, which asks: "Why is it that we want to live longer?" Do we want to extend our life span so that we may in truth bring greater joy and help in the lives of others? Do we want to grow in our ability to give and raise the spirit within ourselves and share that with others in need? Then let us begin and set about this quest for the Fountain of Youth within.

We are often told that of the Ten Commandments, only one is given with a promise: "Honor thy father and thy mother: that thy days may be long upon the land." (Ex. 20:12) How does honoring father and mother relate to the extension of one's life in the earth? If we allow father and mother to symbolize spirit and earth, then if we honor that which we know of the laws of the spirit and of the earth, our days may be extended. Our father and mother in this symbolic sense surely stand for that which has given birth to what we are at this very moment. Therefore, to honor them means to honor all that we have experienced, learned, and received which has brought us to this present moment in the awakening of our consciousness.

To honor all of those experiences would mean to live in accord with what we have learned and have been given to this point of our awakening. If we will begin to do what we know to do now and seek for the next step, we may be assured of finding the path that will lead us to the goal of our quest.

But where shall we begin?

Turn within . . . For, remember, thy body is the temple; there He has promised to meet thee. There ye may commune with Him—NOT outside! That from the outside must answer to that within. What is thy relationship to Him?

2067–6

PART SIX
RELIGION AND
SPIRITUAL
PSYCHOLOGY

Chapter Twenty-Four

EDGAR CAYCE, CHRISTIANITY, AND THE OCCULT

These are times in which it is becoming more and more important that we be very clear about the spiritual foundations of our lives. We need to be more sure about *in whom* we believe and more clear about *what* we believe. For many the Edgar Cayce readings have been very helpful, inspiring a greater commitment and quickening a deeper sense of responsibility to our fellowman.

Yet, for some of us who have found this work so personally helpful, a special problem has arisen; it is trying to integrate our understanding of this information with other sources of spiritual background and insight, such as our study of the Bible or our work with churches. To achieve such an integration, we may have to examine very deeply the true roots or foundations of our spiritual understanding and our spiritual lives. As we set about this course, we may hear the many voices of friends, family, books, ministers, evangelists, rabbis, and priests. To whom should we listen and why? Do they bring us the true spirit or is it merely their own opinion? By what criteria shall we make our evaluations?

In this context let us consider Edgar Cayce. He was a Christian by every criterion of evaluation. He came from a family background which was Christian; his childhood training and experiences were related to the Bible, the church, and his experiences with Jesus. His personal faith and trust were in Jesus. His frequent reading of the Bible and his participation in church activities made his daily activities Christian. The fact that he read the Bible, from cover to cover, every year of his life is quite unique. He always taught a Sunday school class. His personal life was one of self-sacrifice. The content of his life work, the Edgar Cayce readings, is deeply and always Christ-centered, supporting the ultimate importance of the unique work of Jesus of Nazareth.

Edgar Cayce did not make any excessive claims or strong proselytizing efforts regarding the nature of the information he gave in his life work. He simply said that if it might be helpful, give it a try; if not, leave it alone. He sought to serve those who were seeking help. People came from various denominations and religions, or they professed no religion at all; yet, throughout his life, Cayce's emphasis was on helping not converting. And he was also characteristically Christian in how he faced many difficulties in his personal life.

Why then, we may ask, if the life and work of Edgar Cayce were Christian by all of these criteria, is he not widely accepted by Christians of our time? Ostensibly, we may answer that Edgar Cayce's work has been rejected because he spoke of concepts, such as reincarnation, which have not recently been a portion of most Christian teachings. However, we should look more deeply at the history of our religious heritage, if we wish to understand more fully. Is it not frequently the case that throughout the Judeo-Christian tradition, there has been a rejection by people in positions of religious leadership of those spiritually-attuned teachers and prophets who called for a new integrity and a new growth in faith? Thus, the Old Testament prophets, the New Testament apostles, and Jesus Himself were rejected by the religious leaders of their times.

Now we find many people rejecting this new challenge to spiritual growth offered by the Cayce readings. Yet all of the detractors of Edgar Cayce's work have acknowledged the great measure of accuracy and helpfulness in the physical diagnoses and treatment procedures that he gave. Such acknowledgement was based on incontrovertible facts of his life story and the wit-

ness of thousands of people, attesting to the usefulness and applicability of his work.

Nevertheless, Cayce's detractors alleged that the good
work he appears to have done, was a guise assumed
by satanic forces for the purpose of deceiving those
who would seem, initially, to have benefited by the
information. But it may be instructive for us to consider that this was precisely the same accusation
made against Jesus by the religious leaders of His
time.

> Then was brought unto him one possessed with a
> devil, blind, and dumb: and he healed him, insomuch
> that the blind and dumb both spake and saw. And all
> the people were amazed, and said, Is not this the son
> of David? But when the Pharisees heard it, they said,
> This fellow doth not cast out devils, but Beelzebub the
> prince of the devils. And Jesus knew their thoughts,
> and said unto them, Every kingdom divided against
> itself shall not stand: And if Satan cast out Satan, he
> is divided against himself; how shall then his king-
> dom stand? And if I by Beelzebub cast out devils, by
> whom do your children cast them out? therefore they
> shall be your judges, But if I cast out devils by the
> Spirit of God, then the kingdom of God is come unto
> you. Or else how can one enter into a strong man's
> house, and spoil his goods, except he first bind the
> strong man? and then he will spoil his house. He that
> is not with me is against me; and he that gathereth
> now with me scattereth abroad. Wherefore I say unto
> you, All manner of sin and blasphemy shall be for-
> given unto men: but the blasphemy against the Holy
> Ghost shall not be forgiven unto men. And whosoever
> speaketh a word against the Son of man, it shall be
> forgiven him; but whosoever speaketh against the Holy
> Ghost, it shall not be forgiven him, neither in this
> world, neither in the world to come. Either make the
> tree good, and his fruit good; or else make the tree
> corrupt and his fruit corrupt, for the tree is known by
> his fruit.
>
> Matthew 12:22–33

Let us examine thoroughly Jesus' response to this accusation in Matthew 12 that he was performing the work of the devil. Here we find Jesus doing good work. Yet, the religious leaders of His time are uncomfortable with His manner of working and, since His way is not in their organization nor of their persuasion, they are accusing Him of doing good works out of the power of Satan. He, in turn, says that this kind of accusation does not make sense; that a house divided against itself cannot stand, and that a good tree will bear good fruit and a bad tree, bad fruit.

It is also very important for us to observe that it is in this context Jesus teaches about the seriousness of blasphemy against the Holy Ghost. If Edgar Cayce did, in fact, do a good work as all of his detractors acknowledge, then it was a work quickened by the Holy Ghost; and if it is attributed to the devil, then the critic of it may indeed find himself in a position of blasphemy against the Holy Ghost. Therefore, those who become critical of the origin and purpose of a work may claim to speak from the Spirit, and yet, by their criticism, be blaspheming the very work of the Spirit!

How are we to understand, then, such a state of affairs? One of the main problems in all religious and spiritual developments has been differentiating that which is truly of the Spirit, and thus valuable, and that which is a matter of form or tradition. Always when the Spirit works in the earth it is in the context of some form, but it is not necessarily a confirmation of the rightness of that form. If a person experiences a religious conversion or feels that he has been "born again" because of a certain religious experience, he may assume that since the experience was valid, it necessarily follows that all of the doctrines and teachings of that church or that group in which the experience occurred are also valid.

Much rejection of the Edgar Cayce readings has been based on ignorance of what the readings actually say, ignorance of what this work is about, and a serious bias rather than a clear and Spirit-guided understanding.

Now, many Christians today are also worried about Satanic influences and about the destructive potential of what may be called occultism. The Edgar Cayce readings, too, are very concerned with precisely these considerations, but they also give a great deal of information that is helpful in clarifying these important spiritual questions and problems. They point out differences in the mystical, the occult, and the psychic. The *mystical* experience is *the awareness of Oneness.* The *occult* is defined in the readings as *the use of the mind's powers without respect to purposes.* The *psychic* is, according to the readings, *of the soul,* and the preferred terminology regarding the Spirit working through the individual and manifesting its gifts. However, when taken alone, any one of these three terms may become confusing.

Let us consider the readings' definition of occultism, which is the use of the mind's powers without respect to purposes. By this definition, many practices not ordinarily labeled "occult" might be understood to be occult in their true nature. A commonplace example of this is the practice of visualizing certain conditions to be manifested. For example, if you are going into town to do some shopping, you might visualize a parking place on exactly the street where you would like to park. If the mind is used to reserving such a parking place without respect to purpose, this might be called an occult practice. Contrast the difference between determining with your mind that there should be a place for you, with the prayer, "Lord, if I may have such a parking place, let it be so; however, if another is in greater need, then not my will, but Thine." The latter recognizes both the place of the mind and the working of a spiritual law, as well as establishes a priority of purpose by placing our neighbors' needs and our own in proper perspective.

What differentiates between the occult and the spiritual is not the form, nor the organization nor the dogma, but rather the individual's ideals and purposes.

Thus, even though we extol the power of positive thinking, if such is used for our own gain without respect to spiritual purposes or the needs of others, it may be an unwitting practice of occultism, at least in terms of the definition provided by the readings.

Now we might ask, what should our attitude be toward that which we experience as evil? The teachings of Jesus are very clear on this point: first, "Resist not evil." (Matthew 5:39); second, "Love your enemies." (Matthew 5:44); and third, "Judge not, that ye be not judged." (Matthew 7:1). In other words, we should dwell upon and apply the positive and not criticize or attack the negative. Furthermore, it is very clear with respect to the positive, that the ideal of Jesus is the great commandment: to love God with all our heart, mind, and soul, and our neighbor as ourselves.

When Christians or anyone else begin to oppose others just because their ideas are different, then instead of aiding others out of a spirit of love, they have moved away from the very ideal of the Christ. If we ourselves come upon such criticism, and fail to respond to it in a helpful and loving way, then we place ourselves in exactly the same position of judging as those who are critical of us. In our evaluations we must return to the criterion of Jesus: "By their fruits ye shall know them." And the fruits of the spirit, as given in Galatians 5:22, are love, joy, peace, long-suffering, gentleness, goodness, faith, meekness, and temperance. If the spirit of the Christ is present, then these will be the fruit manifested in our attitudes toward one another.

In criticizing others' works because they dare to have different ideas, we may place ourselves in a position of committing the most serious of sins, that is, blasphemy against the Holy Spirit. What does this mean for us personally? It means that if a work is inspired by the Spirit and we deny it, we cut ourselves off from the aid that would have otherwise been available to us through that manifestation of the Spirit.

We need to be clearer about the nature of our loyalties. Is our loyalty to a denomination or a teaching, a belief system, a leader, an attitude, or an approach? Or, is our focus more properly on the ideal that has been set? In one magnificent discourse the Cayce readings trace the whole problem of mankind and present a marvelous solution.

With the present conditions, then, that exist—these (groups and nations) have all come to that place in the development of the human family where there must be a reckoning, a one point upon which all may agree, that out of all of this turmoil that has arisen from the social life, racial differences, the outlook upon the relationship of man to the Creative Forces or his God, and his relationships one with another, must come to some common basis upon which all may agree. You say at once, such a thing is impractical, impossible! What has caused the present conditions, not alone at home but abroad? It is that realization that was asked some thousands of years ago, "Where is thy brother? His blood cries to me from the ground!" and the other portion of the world has answered, is answering, "Am I my brother's keeper?" The world, as a world—that makes for the disruption, for the discontent—has lost its ideal. Man may not have the same *idea*. Man—*all* men—may have the *same IDEAL*.

As the Spirit of God once moved to bring peace and harmony out of chaos, so must the Spirit move over the earth and magnify itself in the hearts, minds and souls of men to bring peace, harmony and understanding, that they may dwell together in a way that will bring that peace, that harmony, that can only come with all having the *one Ideal;* not the one *idea*, but "Thou shalt love the Lord thy God with all thine heart, thy neighbor as thyself!" This (is) the whole law, this (is) the whole answer to the world, to each and every soul. That is the answer to the world conditions as they exist today.

How shall this be brought about? As (they) each in their own respective sphere put into action that they know to be the fulfilling of that as has been from the beginning, so does the little leaven leaven the whole lump.

3976—8

Chapter Twenty-Five

RELIGION AND SPIRITUALITY

The terms religion and spirituality can be used to draw attention to some very special and important considerations differentiating the roles of form and spirit within our lives. We are now using the word religion to refer to forms and structures such as organizations, belief systems, dogmas, constructs, rituals, and procedures; and we are using the word spirituality to refer to the one energy of God, the life force, and to the motivational qualities of the individual who gives expression to this force.

As we examine further the essence of what we are presently calling spiritual, we are working with the premise of *the oneness of all force.* This force is the Spirit, and *the Spirit is life.* This one force of the Spirit is not a neutral force but a force for life, light, and love; and as this force quickens us as individuals, it becomes specifically related to our motivations, to our ideals and purposes, to our intentions, desires and incentives, and to the spirit in which we do whatever we do. If the one spirit is love, then its true work flowing through us will manifest in attitudes and actions demonstrating love.

Religion as Form and Structure

What is the essence of what we are calling religion? Here we are referring to religious structures of the different religions of the world within each of their various denominations. We are also referring to the procedures of these groups. All have certain ways of going about their work—some by television preaching, some by community ministries, some by publications. We are also referring to worship procedures, rituals, and formats for relationships among their members. Further, we are referring to the formal aspects of creeds, dogmas, doctrines, and belief systems.

Many people confuse being religious with being spiritual. Some think that in being religious they are being spiritual. Yet sometimes our religion cuts off rather than enhances the flow of the spirit. On the other hand, many people think they can be more spiritual without any of the limiting factors of religious forms. By rejecting *form*, however, they cut themselves off from the very spirit which they seek. In our life experience both form and spirit are required in proper relationship, one to the other. The problem arises when our stress upon the importance of one limits the role of the other.

Spirit versus Form

Our discussion has been concerned with differentiating the terms *spirit* and *structure*. Let us look at these terms in the context of one of the major premises in the readings: "The spirit is the life, mind is the builder, the physical is the result." Our earth experience has been described as three-dimensional. One of these three dimensions is *space*, and in the dimension of space there appear manifestations variously described as form, materiality, projection, and structure. We may say, then, as a general rule, that when the one reality, the Spirit, the one force, manifests in the earth plane, it will always be experienced in some form or patterning.

The problem then evolves over the role of spirit versus form. On the one hand, if we deny the importance of form, we deny the very vehicle through which the spirit may express in the earth. On the other hand, if we inflate form or cling to it, we may cut off the flow of

the very spirit we seek. Spirit and form are both necessary in our spiritual growth in the earth plane.

If we inflate form we may concern ourselves too much
with matters of concepts, ideas, belief systems, dogmas, doctrines, organizations, rituals, techniques, procedures, policies, and traditions. We may become so
concerned with our religion that we cut ourselves off
from the spirit which would give life to that religion.
We fail then to make attunement with the divine within, and we fail to give expression to the spirit in guided
service to others.

On the other hand, if we deny form because of our
misgivings about this or that organization, we may cut
ourselves off from a specific opportunity, occasion, and
place in which to give expression to the Spirit in service
to others. If we deny form, we may cut ourselves off
from aiding structures, such as the church or syna-
gogue, which have the specific and avowed purpose in
the world to contribute to the good of mankind.

If we have been disappointed by certain religious
structures and teachings, or by such structures and
teachings in general, and thereby abandon them, we
cut ourselves off from spiritual heritages in which many
great souls in this plane and beyond are involved. We
cut ourselves off from the opportunities of long-term
growth in a spiritual community with others who may
have ideals similar to our own, even if their ideas are
different. We cut ourselves off from opportunities for
fellowship. We cut off opportunities for our children to
learn both formally, as in Sunday School classes, and
informally in related activities with their peers who are
addressing themselves to the same spiritual considerations, even if reluctantly and indirectly.

Many times, as we come to see that there is truth in
all teachings, we withdraw from a growing participation in a specific teaching. If we try to embrace all lines
of study for their general value and thereby avoid over-
estimating any particular one, we may become dilet-
tantes skimming the surface. Thus we rob ourselves of

the deeper growth which pursuing specific teachings could offer.

Perhaps we have expected not only too much but also the wrong kinds of things from what religious structures can offer. There is a tendency in mankind to seek to belong to *the* special organization or church that will *assure* us salvation. We seek special techniques that will guarantee results in meditation. We engage in special rituals, by which, if the form is pursued, we may be assured of being made right with God. This quest for the perfect form, the perfect ritual, the perfect organization or the perfect mantra has continued for centuries, indeed thousands of years; it appears to be a chronic propensity for all of mankind.

Yet the truth should be apparent to all—there is no form guaranteeing the spirit of God awakening us. It is clear that two people, side by side, could be engaging in any activity, whether it be organizational, ritual, or apparent service to others, and that one might have a right spirit about this and the other the opposite. Two men may be working in the field; one may be taken up by the Spirit, and the other left. And, clearly, it is the spirit in which the work is done and not the action alone that counts. But how can the Spirit be expressed if there is not a formal act? "For as the body without the spirit is dead, so faith without works is dead also."

(James 2:26)

Diversity and Divinity

Edgar Cayce, in making a strong distinction between *ideas* and *ideals*, says that we cannot all have the same idea but we *must* all have the same *ideals*. One day all souls associated with this solar system must hold to the *one ideal*. However, even at that glorious time there will, of God's own nature, be many ideas.

On one occasion Edgar Cayce was asked how readings should be presented to those of orthodox faith and what should be the approach to those who have become interested in cults and isms? He said the attitude should be "Come and see!" And he further answered regarding both:

> In that same manner; for what is the difference? As he has given, it will ever be found that Truth whether in this or that schism or ism or cult—is of the One Source. Are there not trees of oak, of ash, of pine? There are the needs of these for meeting this or that experience. Hast thou chosen any one of these to be the *all* in thine usages, in thine own life?
> Then, all will fill their place. Find not fault with *any*, but rather show forth as to how good a pine, or ash, or oak, or *vine* thou art!
>
> 254-87

This reading clearly does not invite us to change our organization or affiliation but rather to *be* the very best with respect to the highest ideals and purposes that are properly our own. The problem is not in there being different ideas and beliefs, but rather in what these may lead to if they foster narrowness, exclusiveness, and holier-than-thou attitudes toward others. Is it loving to hold a dogmatic position, the belief in which we require of others? Or is it loving to hold a judgmental attitude toward others who do not share our own ideals? Any orientation that leads to the separateness of a we-they consciousness is clearly not born of love for our fellowman. As we judge others, we cut off the flow of the spirit, and we become less effective in our work even if we think of it as being spiritual.

As a countermeasure to some of the problems that grow out of the narrowness of dogmatism, some of us have rejected all organizations, structures, or belief systems. In so doing, we frequently place ourselves in a position of still greater alienation. But if we think ourselves superior to those who have close organizational affiliations or rigid belief systems, we place ourselves under our own judgment and may reflect an even narrower position by implying that all who do not believe as we do personally are wrong.

We need to view our religious organizations more as opportunities to serve and to build love than as places where people agree upon ideas or concepts, or upon how the organization should be managed. Yet, we may also wonder, even if there *is* a place for so many different organizations and teachings, why is there so little cooperation among them?

If we would keep in mind the uniqueness of the individual even in this lifetime, the great variety of different experiences that each person goes through, adding to that the uniqueness each individual soul may have accrued over many lifetimes, we would surely understand how improbable and unnecessary it is for all to have exactly the same point of view. If mankind is ever to come to love his neighbor, as the great commandment requires, then it must be a love born of sharing the same ideals, not the same ideas. If we truly come to understand and appreciate the reality of the Divine in every soul, then our love of our neighbor becomes straightforward. There is no way that we can simultaneously see God in our neighbor and also hate him.

In addition to the uniqueness of every individual experience, we must understand that God always works through imperfect channels. The authenticity for an individual of a great calling or a great mystical, spiritual, or religious *experience* does not guarantee that the *belief system* of the recipient is necessarily true. No matter how life-transforming such an experience may be, the individual is not necessarily thereby perfected. His experience occurs within the framework of a certain time, a certain country, a certain culture, certain cultural values, certain limitations of language and individual background.

Just because a person is a great spiritual leader, and even nationally or internationally effective, does not necessarily mean that all of his ideas, utterances, or affiliations are thereby given the stamp of approval by the Spirit over and against all other ideas and organizations.

True Spirituality and Form

The basis of spirituality in the individual is motivation. Right motivation is pursued by establishing our spiritual ideals. These will be different for each individual; yet one day all of us must set our ideal in the great commandment. The basis for all motivation must be our love of God and our neighbor as ourselves. This spirit of infinite love abides in us only as we give specific, finite, unique expression to it in our daily lives. As we see and come to love this process in the manifestations of the Spirit in all of the finite forms of nature about us, we may come to see and appreciate the role of form as the vehicle of the Spirit in our own lives.

Chapter Twenty-Six

GOOD AND EVIL

The clearly articulated philosophy of the Edgar Cayce readings is a thoroughgoing monism. Frequently this source of information calls our special attention to the necessity of examining and keeping in mind this first premise: the oneness of all force. There is only one force, and this force is called the Spirit or God. It is not a neutral force. It is good. Moreover, God is love, God is law, God is life. The one force, the Spirit, is life, law, and love.

With the premise of the oneness of all force we affirm that *God is,* that he is *all that is,* and *all that is,* is God. Now when we come to the question of evil there are typically three ways with which we can deal with it: we may elevate evil to a primary premise and thus become dualistic, affirming two realities; we may deny the existence of evil and say that it is the misperception of a lower state of awareness; or we may affirm the reality of evil, but assume it to be contained within the far greater Reality of the first premise of the oneness of all force. The latter of these is clearly suggested in the text from Job in which we are told that, "The sons of God came before the Lord, and Satan came also among them." (Job 1:6)

A summary sketch of the origin of man from the Edgar Cayce readings will enable us to put the nature of evil into proper context. Before the beginning, because we as souls are citizens of eternity, not just temporality, all of us as spiritual beings were perfect and in one accord with the Father. Some of us, in a spirit of rebellion, wanting to be gods apart from God, went astray. With our qualities of being cocreators with the Divine and of having free wills with which to choose, we began to use the one force in creative manifestations which was out of accord with the Whole. We turned away from the light and in our own shadows experienced the darkness. What followed is a very complex story. Much misunderstanding regarding the nature of good and evil has resulted from trying to deal with this in terms far too simplistic for the actual events.

Dimensions of Consciousness and Reality

One of the problems has been in defining the loci or sites wherein we may have experiences in consciousness. Simplistically, we have thought in terms of three or four at most: heaven, hell, earth, and perhaps purgatory. A more adequate understanding requires consideration that there may be many dimensions of consciousness. Another overly simplistic view has been that there was God in heaven, his children who fell in the earth, and perhaps God has a host of angels some of whom reside with Him in heaven and the rest with Satan, as their leader, in hell. With the understanding that there are many dimensions of consciousness, we may also consider that the group of souls who fell out of accord with the whole may have moved to different levels of consciousness and become relatively entrapped.

Many of us who have come to be comfortable in addressing and considering the facts of reincarnation, have still not prepared ourselves to contemplate the nature of our experiences in other dimensions *between* incarnations. But the Edgar Cayce readings indicate that there are many dimensions of consciousness into which we may move for the purpose of experiencing their various attributes. Thus we are confronted with the question of the way in which these dimensions are peopled or populated.

Even if we are comfortable with the concept of angels, we may be disinclined to think extensively of the various types of angels and their assignments, of the planes of consciousness in which they work, or of the extent which they may be in or out of accord with the One Spirit. These considerations imply a kind of hierarchy in the spirit world. The Bible implies it, the readings confirm it, and many reputable esoteric sources develop the concept of a hierarchy extensively.

The readings suggest that although there is a hierarchy, our attitude should not be to make this hierarchy our ideal, reflecting our purpose. Nor should we try to communicate with these hierarchies and helpful beings. Rather, our orientation and trust should be directly to God. If He sends a messenger, that is good; but each of us should seek to become a direct channel through which may pass the application of the fatherhood of God, the brotherhood of man, and the universal Christ–Consciousness.

Hierarchy of Evil

Today many New Thought or New Age thinkers have come to accept a notion of other dimensions, of other spirit beings, and of each individual having his own spirit guide. However, some of these thinkers still have great difficulty in contemplating a hierarchy whose purposes are *not* constructive, in the same way that there may be a hierarchy of those whose purposes are in accord with the One Force.

The sleeping Cayce was once asked to explain the popular concept of the Devil in relationship to the One-ness of all force, as seemingly substantiated by many passages in the Bible. He responded:

> In the beginning, celestial beings. We have first the Son, then the other sons or celestial beings that are given their force and power. Hence that force which rebelled in the unseen forces (or in spirit), that came into activity, was that influence which has been called Satan, the Devil, the Serpent, they are One. That of rebellion!
>
> Hence, when man in any activity rebels against the influences of good he harkens to the influence of evil rather than the influences of good. . . . Evil is rebellion, God is the Son of Life, of Light, of Truth; and the Son of Light, of Life, of Truth, came into physical being to demonstrate and show and lead the way for man's ascent to the power of good over evil in a material world. As there is, then, a personal savior, there is the personal devil.
>
> 262–52

What about this influence referred to as the spirit of rebellion and variously called Satan, the Devil, the Serpent? Is this only a quality of spirit or does it represent a specific individual? The readings refer to Satan, Lucifer, the Devil as a *soul*. In the Bible the book of Job refers to "the sons of God (who) came to present themselves before the Lord and Satan came also among them." The personal identity of this soul, this being, is referred to many times throughout the readings.

So how shall we put together in summary fashion a story that makes sense about the relationship of the spirit of evil and angelic beings who have fallen, and that one whom we know as Satan, Lucifer, or the Devil? We are told in the readings that man's rebellion and consorting with others for personal aggrandizement first brought Satan, or the Serpent, into Eden. Did Satan cause the desire or did the desire invite the entering of Satan?

The cosmic scenario might go something like this: In the beginning all beings were created perfect and were in a perfect accord with God. A portion of these, only a portion, went astray. Those who went astray became involved in various dimensions of reality. Because as souls we are cocreators with God, our very thoughts became creations and those who were astray created thought forms out of accord with the whole. These thought forms became so entangling that those souls did not even know that they were cutoff from an awareness of their oneness with the whole. Thus it became God's quest to bring these souls back into a remembrance of their divine heritage and into full accord with Him. To do so required an array of experiences in consciousness so that they could become aware of their separation. As Satan is permitted a role in the story of Job, so some souls out of accord with the whole began to play a role in this awakening of others. This work, while having a salutary effect, was nevertheless a kind of rebellion and self-aggrandizement, and thus out of accord with the full nature of the love of God.

We can see clearly in our earth plane experience that there are many who set about deliberately to do evil or injury to their fellowman. This may be by deception, theft, or assault. We also see clearly that on occasion those with such intents and purposes band together and as a group attack other individuals or groups. We see, too, how some of those who band together form an extraordinary power structure and hierarchy of leadership. Hitler in Germany was such an example. The Mafia is another, with its highly structured hierarchy organized for the commission of crime.

When in death we pass through God's other door, there may be little change in our consciousness or motivation. Therefore, if there is an organized hierarchy of those bent on evil in the earth plane, then how would it be surprising to us that there might be such a hierarchy in the spirit plane!

Power of the One Force

While recognizing the reality of evil and the fact that there are individuals with evil intents and purposes, we should not elevate these facts to a primary premise, thereby hypothesizing a dualistic philosophy of good and evil. There is only One Force. God is the Father of all, and all of us here are among those gone astray.

Now what power have these evil influences been given over us? *None*, except what we in our own thoughts, desires, and indiscretions open ourselves to. We make ourselves vulnerable by getting out of attunement physically, mentally, and spiritually. As we seek expressions or activities that are out of accord, we attune our vibrations to lower consciousness much as we would attune a radio to a certain station. By physical imbalances we sometimes open ourselves to other influences. Some of these influences may be from other entities. More frequently these influences are our own thought forms energized. Sometimes there is actual possession by another entity.

What determines the sources that affect us as individuals whether from a physical, mental, or spirit plane? That which opens us to the influence is our purpose, the motivative force, the intent, and desire. Out of our desire we can be in attunement with the Infinite. Out of desire we can invoke the presence of Jesus. Out of our desire, if it be of selfishness, or self-aggrandizement, we may open ourselves to influences that are motivated by that same lower quality of intention.

The Cayce readings further indicate that there are countless entities in the spirit plane who, not taking cognizance of their present state, still want to have a say in the affairs of the world. If we open ourselves to concerns about what others think, we open ourselves to the influences of the vibrations of those consciousnesses. The effects of telepathic rapport and of prayer are examples of this.

Once again it is the ideal being held by the individ-

ual that sets the vibration. Again we stress and under-
line the challenge from the readings that the most
important experience for any entity is to know what is
the ideal spiritually.

> What then is thy ideal? In WHOM have ye believed,
> as well as in what have ye believed? Is that in which
> thou has believed able to keep ever before thee that
> thou committest unto Him? Yes—through thy angel,
> through thy SELF that IS the angel—does the self
> speak with thy Ideal.
>
> 1646–1

Heaven and Hell

Concerning the question of heaven and hell, it is
clear from the readings that these refer primarily to
states of consciousness. Heaven is an awareness of our
oneness with the Father; thus, we do not go to heaven,
we grow to heaven, for each soul grows to the awareness within the temple of its own body. As we experience being away from the at—oneness, this state is
called hell.

The question of heaven and hell relates also to a
consideration of the concept of reincarnation. Some
feel that reincarnation eliminates notions of heaven
and hell as the soul, through successive experiences,
grows in its greater awareness of its oneness with
God. However, there is also a spatial dimension to
these movements in consciousness related not only
to other planets and dimensions but also to other solar
systems.

Some living exemplary lives in terms of purposes and
actions of helpfulness and selflessness toward their
fellowman may indeed free themselves of desires that
would attract them again to the earth. Others may
express the desire to never again incarnate without
having purified their desires in such a way as to be
truly free from the carnal influences. Thus the readings say:

. . . though a soul may will itself never to reincarnate, but must burn and burn and burn or suffer and
suffer and suffer! For, the heaven and hell is built by
the soul.

5753–1

Thus we see that even if the entity does not incarnate again there may be elements of desire remaining,
and as those desires are unfulfilled, they give the discarnate soul the experience of burning, due to unfulfilled desire.

Summary

The real evil is the spirit of rebellion. When we entertain that spirit within ourselves, we open ourselves to
influences with similar motives. Do we not say, "Speak
of the devil and he will appear?" What does this mean?
It means that if we have the consciousness of evil, then
evil is present with us. We say we believe in God. Then
let us put our trust in God. Why entertain others when
He is so high?

He that dwelleth in the secret place of the most
High shall abide under the shadow of the Almighty. I
will say of the Lord, He is my refuge and my fortress:
my God, in him will I trust. . . . There shall no evil
befall thee. . . . For he shall give his angels charge
over thee, to keep thee in all thy ways.

Psalm 91

Chapter Twenty-Seven
JESUS WHO BECAME THE CHRIST

The work of Edgar Cayce has attracted hundreds of
thousands of people representing a wide range of religious interests and backgrounds. Many who came to

him were troubled over religious questions. Edgar Cayce encouraged comparative study. He frequently stated that we learn by comparing different points of view, for "No finite mind can hold all the truth." As he suggests, our fellowmen are always going to have experiences, awarenesses, and therefore viewpoints different from our own. If we can listen to each other and share our experiences, we have a chance to broaden our insights.

The Universal Viewpoint

First, let us consider the universal outlook so frequently expressed in the readings. The basis for such an all-inclusive outlook is the premise that God is the Father of us all, that all of us spiritual beings, are His children; and, that as spiritual beings we have a continuity of life not only forward into eternity, but in a preexistence of this incarnation back to the beginning.

From these readings we may begin to see how reincarnation is not only a fact but an extremely important working concept for us in understanding ourselves, others, and our relationship to them. We may thus truly see the brotherhood of all nations, of all religions, and of all people. We may come to understand that we ourselves have been perhaps Hindu, Buddhist, Moslem, Taoist, Christian, and Jew. The concept of reincarnation is the great leveller—it makes mankind heirs of the great persons of history. Buddha does not belong only to Buddhists, but to all mankind. Jesus does not belong only to Christians but to all mankind. Moses does not belong only to the Jews, nor Gandhi only to Hindus. These spiritual leaders enrich the spiritual heritage of all humankind.

Cayce warned us:

. . . he that declares as a name, in a name, save in the universality of the Father, limits the ability of the seeker, (and) of the channel through which that glory may come to any.

Learn, rather, that given: 'By what name shall I say that I am sent?' I AM THAT I AM. That, rather than any name of this, that or the other manner. The I AM that seeks gain, then, that access to the I AM that brought, brings, holds, the worlds in their place.

254-85

A thirty-nine-year-old Jewish rabbi received a life reading from Mr. Cayce. He was told that his previous incarnation was in early America as a French Catholic trader. Before that he was among the children of Israel in the Old Testament times, and before that a Zoroastrian in Persia. He asked if he should remain a rabbi, and was told:

Yes, as a rabbi in its *truest* sense; that is—a teacher, a minister. Not as bound by any creeds! Not as bound by modes! Not as bound by any law!

Coordinate the teachings, the philosophies of the East and the West, the oriental and the occidental, the new truths and the old. . . . Correlate not the differences, but where all religions meet—THERE IS ONE GOD! 'Know, O Israel, the Lord thy God is *ONE*!'

. . . Hast thou not found that the essence, the truth, the real truth is one. Mercy, justice, peace, harmony. For without Moses and his leader, Joshua, (that was bodily Jesus) there is no Christ. Christ is not a man; Jesus was the man, Christ the messenger. Christ in all ages, Jesus in one, Joshua in another, Melchizedek in another. These be those that led Judaism. These be they that came as that child of promise is in thee that ye lead as He has given thee, 'Feed my sheep.'

991-1

As we contemplate the preexistence of Jesus who said in the New Testament, "Before Abraham was, I am" (John 8:58), we may seriously study the Cayce reading which suggests a relationship between Jesus and the founding fathers of Judaism. As the readings point to a relationship between Joshua and Jesus, the

Bible suggests that when Moses spoke face-to-face with the Lord, Joshua was with him in a very special way.

> It came to pass as Moses entered into the tabernacle, the cloudy pillar descended, and stood at the door of the tabernacle, and the Lord talked with Moses . . . face-to-face as a man speaketh unto his friend. And he turned again into the camp: but his servant Joshua, the son of Nun, a young man, departed not out of the tabernacle.
>
> Exodus 33:9, 11

The readings indicate that the spirit of Christ was with the Buddha in his meditations, that this Spirit manifested in the high priest, Melchizedek, and in the service aspects of Joshua. This same Christ Spirit *took up* the life of the man Jesus completely. Wherever there has been the teaching of the One God, the Spirit of the Christ has been present; and wherever there has been a need of mankind, He has been working. Thus, we are told in the Old Testament prophecy of His coming to be born in Bethlehem:

> Out of thee shall He come forth unto me that is to be the ruler in Israel; whose goings forth have been from the old, from everlasting.
>
> Micah 5:2

When we come to understand the oneness of all mankind and the universality of God's love for His children, we may then contemplate the oneness of that toward which the religions of the world seek. The Buddhists anticipate the coming of Maitreya, the Jews seek the Messiah, and the Christians look forward to the Second Coming. There can be little doubt that the sooner we all sense the oneness of what we seek in the coming manifestation of God in the earth, the sooner those hopes will be fulfilled for us all. There is the likelihood that they will be fulfilled by *One*, which all might claim as their own, but when He is fully seen we will also see the Oneness instead of the differences which exist in our present attitudes.

Jesus Who Became the Christ

There is a continuing emphasis in the Edgar Cayce readings on the premise of Oneness and on the attitude of inclusiveness rather than exclusiveness. And there are also many references pointing to the special relationship of Jesus to the Christ and of that relationship to the One Force. The serious student will want to read, reread, and reflect again on the exact wording of this information.

We find in the readings the expression, "Jesus who became the Christ," and the statement that "The Spirit of the Christ took up the life of the man Jesus." Apparently, in being fully obedient to the law, He became the Law. The messenger became the Message. The life, death, and resurrection were the completion of the project undertaken with the manifestation of Adam and Eve in the earth plane. With the coming of Adam, what had been made in the image of God, the souls of us all, had a temple in which to come to an awareness of that oneness while still in the earth plane. Next, the pattern of the image of God, written in all our souls, had to become lived out in the life of man. As Jesus fully lived out this pattern, He *became* the pattern and the ideal, the standard for us all. The Christ is the *power*—Jesus is the *pattern*.

To understand the special significance of this event, we must consider more exactly the way in which we as souls were cut off from God. We were made to be cocreators with Him and thus as we experience our beingness, our thoughts became creations. What we *thought*, we *became*. We built thought forms which cut us off from the awareness of our oneness. It is not primarily our physical body that keeps us from being conscious of our oneness with God. The body is simply the projection of the thought forms that we have built over countless ages. Part of the nature of the lost condition of man is being trapped in thought forms, which stand between our present focal point of consciousness and our oneness with the Infinite.

Jesus, in fulfilling the law, established for all mankind a *new thought form*, a pattern, through which man might enter into an awareness of his oneness with God. He accomplished this against the tremendously overwhelming odds of thought forms and pressures of untold numbers of people throughout the ages. He had to deal with the innumerable thoughts of beings, both incarnate and discarnate who, in their blindness, did not wish to see such an event accomplished.

We ourselves can hardly resist the encouragement of a friend to take another dessert or the discouragement of a friend's criticism, which draws us away from our purposes. Yet Jesus never faltered in His ideal and purpose, even against overwhelming resistance. Despite these odds, by establishing a perfect pattern and a mediating thought form for us all, it may be said that He not only took on the sins of the world but that His life was an atonement for us, a pattern of attaining the awareness of the at-one-ment with God.

The most controversial aspect of contemplating the relationship of Jesus with God is the question of the divine nature of a man. In Jesus we are told that God became incarnate. If we could only see clearly that Jesus' claim for divinity is a claim for the divinity of us all, we would understand that His relationship to God is a pattern which all of us may and one day must attain. Yes, He said, "If ye have seen me, you have seen the Father," but He also said, "I in the Father, the Father in me, I in you, you in me." The principle is that there is only one force, only one spirit. If we will work again and again with the principle of oneness, we can see that as spiritual beings we are to become one with the Father and there is no separation of that Spirit which took up the life of the man Jesus from that Spirit which may bring light and life and love in our own lives.

Jesus manifested this oneness with the Spirit so fully that, in expressing it, the Edgar Cayce readings have a most extraordinary way of showing that special relationship between the macrocosmic Christ and the microcosmic historical life of Jesus of Nazareth. For example the source asked:

> Who was the greatest? He that made the worlds or He that washed His disciples' feet?
>
> 254–55

In the first chapter of the Gospel of John, we are told:

> In the beginning was the Word, and the Word was with God, and the Word was God. . . . All things were made by Him. . . . And the Word was made flesh, and dwelt among us.
>
> John 1: 1,3,14

Thus, the Word or the Logos, is the Christ, that aspect of God which is the builder and through which everything that was made was made. That Christ Spirit then took up the life of the man Jesus and became flesh and dwelt among us.

The difficulty we have with the notion that God can manifest in fullness in a man, is perhaps our own inner resistance to the idea that we ourselves are spiritual beings, gods, who must one day come ourselves to full obedience to the law of love and the full manifestation of our oneness with God. The mission of Jesus was first to establish that pattern, that standard, that ideal, that concrete example in the consciousness of mankind and then to challenge us to measure up to it saying:

> Ye are gods, and all of you are children of the most High.
>
> John 10:34, Psalm 82:6

The Specific Role of Jesus

Since we are all children of the One God, then wherever we are and by whatever name we pray, if we call upon Him, He is responsive. What, then, is the special role of Jesus? And why should we concern ourselves with this Name or with questions of our relationship to Him?

Let us remember that the Judeo–Christian tradition is a tradition of the *word*. God *spoke*, and creation came into being. The earliest commandments warned that we should cherish the name of God and should not take it in vain. The ancient Hebrews guarded the Name so carefully that some would not utter or write it in its fullest form. Part of the wisdom of this may be understood as we contemplate the Eastern concept of *mantra*, the power of a word to call into being a reality. Unless we take special care of these sacred words, they lose their mantric effect upon us. We then have no special expression to awaken within ourselves a consciousness that gives us a true sense of the immanent presence and power of the divine. For some of us, the word *Jesus* may become such a mantra, an ideal, a quickener of the consciousness.

In fulfilling the law, Jesus became the Law. He became the concrete example of love expressed in the earth. He became the fulfillment of that image of God in which all of us as souls are made. He became the standard, the criterion, the measuring rod by which all of us must one day measure ourselves. He has established a thought form accessible to us all which mediates between our present consciousness and the fullness of the Divine. But He represents an aspect of the Divine which is very special—the fullness of the love, of the grace, of the forgiveness, of the joy of the Divine.

There is a function of the Divine that is of the law: law, as we understand it, is the law of karma, that what we sow we shall reap. And there are beings, angelic beings, whose assignment it is to see that these laws are met and fulfilled. Then, how are we to attune ourselves to that aspect of the Divine of which we are all so much in need? How shall we attune ourselves to the life, the love, the healing power, the forgiving grace, and joy of the Divine? What way have we to quicken our consciousnesses to Infinite love? There is a word, a name, which stands above every other name, as it represents the fulfillment of the expression of the Divine in the earth. By this name we may enter in our own consciousness into the holy of holies within, where we may meet God face-to-face. And if we will accept it as such, this name, *Jesus*, may become for us a mantra invoking and inviting that aspect of the Divine which is the love of a Father, who seeks and cares for us and who will supply for us all that which we need.

But there is one thing more. In being fully obedient to the law and thus becoming the Law, Jesus gained mastery over the dimensions of our present consciousness. As He gained mastery over time and space, these are no longer limitations for His manifestation. He may now not only bilocate, as we have heard of some of the masters of old, but He may manifest anywhere, anytime. If we claim His promises that He is with us always, that He will not leave us comfortless, that if we call, He will answer, we may be assured in truth of a companion. He will not only be present with us in place of fear, but He will also mediate for us in our relationships with others, whether incarnate or discarnate, in a consciousness and power that we of ourselves cannot express.

We have in Jesus literally, then, a friend who will come to us as we bid Him in sincerity to enter but who, out of respect for our own free will, will not be the uninvited guest. It is true that God in His love is cognizant of us all; however, in the body of God there are many beings, incarnate, discarnate, and angelic. There are many consciousnesses with which we have to contend. Some of us feel we can make it on our own; others feel we need all the help we can get. It may be that we have built for ourselves karmic patterns, and a vulnerability to the influences of others, so that without such a Friend we are lost indeed. In the Edgar Cayce readings we find encouragement which is surprisingly specific, inviting us all to just that kind of personal relationship with Jesus:

> Take it to Jesus! He IS thy answer. He is Life, Light and Immortality. He is Truth, and is thy elder brother.
>
> 1326—1

> For the Master, Jesus, even the Christ, is the pattern for every man in the earth, whether he be Gentile or Jew, Parthenian or Greek. For all have the pattern, whether they call on that name or not; but there is no other name given under heaven whereby men may be saved from themselves.
>
> 3528—1

The Reappearance of The Christ

It is only by contemplating the implications of reincarnation—that we have existed and incarnated many time heretofore and may indeed exist and incarnate many times to come—that we can conceptualize the magnitude of the work on human nature.

As we gain the greater perspective of what it means that we are spiritual beings created by God in the beginning, we may see that even these experiences in the earth constitute the way He has prepared for us to begin to find our way in consciousness back to the oneness with Him. From the days of Adam and continuing beyond the present, He has set about a work of redeeming the souls of all mankind.

As the readings indicate, nothing truer has ever been spoken than that God is not willing that any soul should perish; consequently He has prepared a way so that every soul may have the experiences it needs to find its way back to that at-one-ment with Him. And so, it may be anticipated that the work will continue until it is fully completed. Remember the good shepherd with ninety-nine sheep in the fold who went after the *one* who was lost. So we may anticipate that He, in His commitment as a Good Shepherd, will continue to work with us and seek after us until all of us return to the fold as children of God and citizens of the Universe.

PART SEVEN
KNOWING THYSELF

Behold, the days come, saith the Lord, that I will make a new covenant with the house of Israel. . . . I will put my law in their inward parts, and write it in their hearts; and will be their God, and they shall be my people . . . for they shall all know me, from the least of them unto the greatest of them, · saith the Lord. . . .

Jeremiah 31:31,33,34

Chapter Twenty-Eight
KNOWING THYSELF

The great question of the East is "Who am I?" In the West the same question takes the form given us by the Psalmist who pondered, "What is man that thou art mindful of him?" All thinking persons ask, "What is the truth? What is the ultimate nature of reality?" and "How can I know for sure?" And all are puzzled by the eternal riddle, "If a man die, shall he live again?" "Why is there pain and suffering?" "How can I better understand myself and others?" and "How can I change so as to become what I know I could be?"

The ancient philosopher said, "Know thyself," and more recently we have been reminded that the proper study of mankind is man. Edgar Cayce said, "The greater study of individuals, groups, nations should be the study of self."

We must either come to know ourselves, or, if we live an unexamined life, we may find that we have devoted our time, our energies, our efforts to endeavors which in retrospect were far afield from what we really knew to be worthwhile and that which we truly wished to accomplish. Not knowing ourselves, we live out our days driven by the pressures of the world, of those about us, and of the immediate desires and tensions of the physical body. We allow habits, addictions, and compulsions to guide our activities rather than our own higher sense of what is right and most valuable for ourself and others. We have given others a power over us—other peoples' thoughts, creeds, expectations, fears, and prejudices. We need to know ourselves, both to *avoid* becoming what we need not be, and to allow ourselves to *become* what we truly are.

In the Beginning

As each of us sets upon the path of knowing self in the deepest and most meaningful sense, where shall we begin? Perhaps the proper place to start is, "In the beginning, *God!*" God is not only philosophically the affirmation of a first premise, but is also personally the establishment of a rock upon which to stand. It is a rock formed from the premise of the *oneness of all force*, which when fully appreciated sheds light upon every conceivable or imaginable consideration.

More consequences for thought and action follow from the affirmation or denial of God than from answering any other fundamental question. Such consequences follow for those who regard the question as answerable only by faith or only by reason; they follow for those who deny; and they follow for those who insist upon suspending judgment entirely. Thus, the first step in coming to know ourselves is to do the hard, solid, clear thinking work of establishing and keeping straight some first premises; "Know O Israel, the Lord thy God is One."

The Edgar Cayce readings as well as other responsible sources provide abundant objective evidence that there are realities all about us beyond our present state of consciousness. The implications of such a Reality should challenge us at the deepest roots of our being to ask, "If there is another reality, might it not be as important or even more important in some respects than the present awareness in which we are so heavily invested?"

If we get the sense of such a Reality and affirm God, the oneness of all force, then we may take the next step and address that which the readings evaluate as the ultimate agenda for all mankind: the *living of the great commandment.* We are to love God with all our heart, mind, and soul, and our neighbor as ourselves. This Edgar Cayce represented as the ideal for all mankind and the answer to all the problems of all mankind. Yet we find ourselves unwilling or unable to live by such a standard. Thus coming to know ourselves is to deal with that part of ourselves which keeps us from becoming what we are.

A major hindrance and barrier to loving God and others lies in the inadequate understanding we have of ourselves, of our basic spiritual nature, of the spiritual nature of others, and of the lawfulness of the influences which have led to our present state with all its limitations and opportunities. We do not understand the forces, structures, and processes involved in the functioning of our total being and in our relationships with others. We lack proper perspective of our ultimate potential. We must come to understand fully that we are spiritual beings and that all of us are children of God.

Our Search for God

In the Bible we are assured that if we will but seek, we shall find. We may consider it to be a universal law that, if we seek, a law is put into action assuring us that we shall indeed find. So let us begin our search for God!* Ours is a time in which there is an abundance of literature, publications, workshops, leaders, and instructors; and, especially important for many of us, access to the Edgar Cayce readings.** If we will but pursue these opportunities and make of them a kind of mental and spiritual food, we may indeed begin to grow. We may learn by comparison, not asking who is right or wrong, but rather allowing the dwelling upon uplifting subject matter to quicken a sense of our own beingness and the potential of expanded awareness, to which we are all heirs.

If we affirm God, we mean not only that God is, but also that He is all that is, and *all that is is God.*

*For information about study groups organized for such a purpose write A.R.E., Box 595, Virginia Beach, Virginia 23451.
**THERE IS A RIVER by Thomas Sugrue, a biography of Edgar Cayce is an excellent introduction for the study of this information.

Affirming God affirms not only Being but that quality of Being which is Love. *God is Love*, and it follows that we are to love Him and His manifestations in creation. The affirmation of God further requires us to consider Love as the motivating force of the universe, and to ask ourselves whether our own motives are in or out of accord with the flow of this force of Love. As children of God, love is also the very nature of our being. As we set love as an ideal, we may begin to awaken its motivational potential within ourselves more and more frequently under more and more conditions.

Many of us have acknowledged the primacy of the Great Commandment but we have not found it in ourselves to make it the motivation, incentive, and criterion for our lives. Since God is Love and He is in the process of bringing all to be in accord with LOVE, we may come to see this Commandment not as an optional moralism but as an ultimate requirement. The law to be fulfilled is the law of Love. We were made in the image of Love; it is our destiny to be conformed to Love. If we set it as our ideal, we may "the sooner" grow into full accord with that Destiny.

As we get a sense that our true origin and our true nature is of the Divine, and that Love is the ideal, we may address the question of why we are not in full command of that divine capability. What stands between us and our full attunement with that potential?

We experience separation in fears, inhibitions, innate dislikes, lack of talent, or desired qualities of character. We experience misunderstandings and disappointments in our relationships with others. We experience disorders or diseases which are irritating or even disabling. We find in ourselves inclinations and tendencies to certain weaknesses of body, mind, and character. Why?

Through the writings of Sigmund Freud we have come to hear the expression, the *unconscious*. No one of us experiences it as being a part of ourselves because by its very nature and definition, it *is* unconscious. We may disavow or ignore the unconscious part of ourselves for a time, but sooner or later it begins to have its effect in our lives, on our bodies, and on our relationships with others.

If, as indicated by the Edgar Cayce readings, we have lived many lives in previous incarnations, the extent of this unconscious within our own personal experiences is vast beyond imagining. And if we add to that the consideration all subconscious minds are in contact, one with another, and if we reflect upon the collective nature of the thought forms of mankind, we further see just how expansive a realm resides on the other side of the door of consciousness. How can we open the door to our unconscious and deal with it?

Turning Within

The extraordinary information given through Edgar Cayce opens for many of us a way, not *the* way, but *a* way to begin to understand ourselves and our unconscious with a depth and richness never before possible. Through this source we are given an understanding of our relationship with all of mankind and with the Divine, which is vast beyond most of mankind's greatest dreams. These readings provide exceptional depth of insight and applicable helpfulness. When applied this information works. With every quickening promise from this source regarding our divine nature and our relationship with the Infinite, we are challenged to day-by-day application of that which we have learned in acts of kindness, patience, gentleness, and helpfulness toward those about us. Here is a teaching which embodies the religions of the world in a universal spirit, and yet challenges us to follow our own inner guidance with respect to our personal relationship to God. And through this information we may learn of an exceptionally applicable approach to an attunement with God.

Although Edgar Cayce gave literally thousands of principles or applications that can be useful in our daily lives, perhaps one of the most important insights given is the insistence that we must all *turn within to meet God*. Just as our eyes are sensitive to light; so is our soul sensitive to God. We may know the God of the Universe only through our own soul, that portion of the divine within the depths of our inner being.

Cayce said that all healing comes from within. No application of any kind is healing of itself, but all of us have within us an access to that Spirit that may bring new life and rejuvenation. When someone asked for help, such as the physical diagnosis of an illness, the Edgar Cayce information was accurate and specific. However, when anyone came, as hundreds did, with questions about decisions or guidance regarding choices, they were told again and again to turn within. He assured them all that no matter how far astray they had gone, they could meet God within the temple of their own bodies.

In the readings we have specific and detailed instructions for attuning the physical and mental to the spiritual. In the process of meditation we can put aside our limitations and move through that vast realm of the unconscious which has been so problematic for so many individuals in dealing with their personal lives. How is it that we can move through these barriers to the greater reality of our being on the other side? Cayce called it "attuning the physical and the mental to the spiritual" truth of ourselves. Not only are we spiritual beings with a direct tie to the Divine, but each one of us has the potential of a perfect pattern for perfect functioning physically, mentally, and spiritually.

Archetypes of the Self

There is a hierarchy of archetypes or patterns of the unconscious. At the top of this hierarchy is the archetype or pattern of the Self. When energized, this pattern brings about a balance and an integration in the individual enabling him to manifest his fullest potential. With this concept we may begin to appreciate the promise of the covenant of old wherein we are told, "I will put my law in their inward parts and write it in their hearts and will be their God and they shall be my people." This law in our inward parts is the *image of God* in which we are made. It is the circuitry or the programming, within our own bodies as temples of the living God, through which we may make attunement with the Divine. As the Spirit energizes this pattern and is permitted to flow through us in application we *become* the image of God, in which we were created in the beginning and to which we are destined to be conformed.

Although the practice of meditation sounds like a technique, its working principle is the living Spirit which flows through us as we attune ourselves and apply that spirit in acts of helpfulness to others. As we pursue the practice of meditation, there is awakened within us remembrances, recollections of past lives and past relationships, hidden talents and potentials for gifts of the spirit which bring a new dimension, a new richness, a new awareness to our lives and to the lives of those with whom we come in contact. Rather than a Pandora's box, the unconscious through meditation becomes an unlimited storehouse of talent when the patterns within it are awakened by the Spirit for the right purpose and at the right times. Stumbling blocks become stepping-stones. Thus, it is only in attunement to the Spirit within that we truly come to know ourselves.

The Truth Awaits Us Within

We were warned by Jesus that in the last days many would come in his name, saying, "I am the Christ." If they would say he is in the desert or he is in the secret chambers, His special warning was, "Go not forth!" There is a psychological principle underlying this teaching: it is to warn against the temptation to turn to others as a source of information, guidance, or healing in preference for and in neglect of the attunement with the Spirit that we can and must make within the temple of our own bodies. Thus Jesus said, "It is expedient for you that I go away; for if I go not away, the Comforter will not come unto you." (John 16:7) In other words, while others may aid, our trust must be in the living God. Anyone can make of any other—whether it be the church, a charismatic movement, the Edgar Cayce readings or the Bible itself—a false prophet if they prefer the fixed external structure to the living spirit within themselves.

The New Covenant, in which we are promised, "They shall know me, from the least of them unto the greatest of them," is preceded by the promise that, "I will put my law in their inward parts, and write it in their hearts." (Jeremiah 31: 34,33) It is clear from this that the way in which we are all to come to know God and the truth of our own selves is by quickening that law written in our inward parts, that pattern of the Christ, that archetype of the Self written on the minds of our souls, that image in which we are made which is the image of God.

The way in which we may awaken this pattern, this archetype of the Self, this Law, is again clearly seen in the necessity first of establishing it as *the ideal*. It must be that which we would hold as the motivating influence in our lives and the standard and criterion by which all decisions and judgments are made. As we set this pattern as the ideal, dwell upon it with the imaginative forces of the mind, and give it the opportunity to be awakened and energized by the daily practice of meditation, then we come truly to know ourselves.

When we are told, "Be still and know," we may come to understand that unless we are still we can never know ourselves. To know the true Self requires that the lower consciousness and the lower self be still and quiet. Then, directed by a high ideal, the imaginative forces of the mind may quicken the Spirit within to flow through the pattern of the true Self. Among the wilderness of the many voices that would tell us what

to do or what to think or what to believe, how to vote
and what we should fear, here is a voice that says,
"Turn within, meet God within the temple of your own
body."

A Little Leaven

The greatest reason for our need to know ourselves is
that we may become greater channels for the expression of the living spirit in helpfulness to others. There
is a world in pain, suffering, and darkness awaiting a
new dawn, a new age, a new consciousness, and the
fulfillment of a new covenant. Every one of us can make
a greater contribution to this need than we tend ever
to imagine. The contribution to be made is not at the
level of governments or agencies or organizations, but
rather in the change within ourselves. Through attunement and application we may become channels through
which the living Spirit may flow. Remember that the
unit through which God may express in the earth is
the individual soul. It is only by changed individuals
that we may have changed groups, organizations, governments, and nations of the world.

The magnitude of this task may seem overwhelming
and staggering. With three of the four billion people
incarnate in the earth today living in poverty, with
some of the nations of the world at war and the greater
nations in preparation for war, with all the political,
economic and social strife, there may seem to be little
promise of a single individual making a true contribution to changing the world. Yet, the arithmetic of this
possibility is straightforward. Remember Edgar Cayce
said this is a work of leavening: "A little leaven leavens
the whole lump." Consider: if only one person, living
such a spirit-quickened life, could change the lives of
ten others, and those ten others changed the lives of a
hundred, and so on. . . . With only ten initial steps of
leavening, we will have eventually exceeded double the
population of the world.

As we look upon these most extraordinary, and for some seemingly insurmountable, times we must remember that God, the maker of the universe and the Father of us all, has made us a New Covenant. We have but to look within to know our true self and to find our true destiny. Let us begin.

INDEX

A

Abraham, 218
acid levels in body, 182–183
action, *See* continuity of action
Adam, 20, 170, 220, 225
adjustments, 167, 180
adrenal glands, 155
Akashic records, 72
alcohol, 182, 187
alkaline levels in body, 182–183
almonds, 183
anabolism, 184
angels, 34, 49, 50, 134, 212
animals, 74–75
apples, 183
application, xii–xiii, 10–18, 111, 118–119
appreciation, sense of, 151, 166
archangels, 34, 35, 46
archetypes, 54–55, 233–234
Arcturus, 31
ARE (Association for Research and Enlightenment), 2, 16, 230n.
Aristotle, 3
ark of the covenant, 41
Armaggedon, battle of, 178
assimilation, 167, 181–183
Association for Research and Enlightenment (ARE), 2, 16, 230n.
astral projections, 46–47, 133
atheism, 80
atoms, 81–82, 165
atonement, 62, 86, 98

attitudes, 113–114, 122–123, 137–138
attraction, law of, 81–82
attunement, 10–18, 46–47, 68–70, 71, 85–86
auric fields, 29–30
autonomic nervous system, 44–45, 63–65, 145
awareness, 111

B

bacon, 182
balance, law of, 81–82
beef, 182, 187
behavior patterns, 123
beingness, 28, 82
beverages, 182–183, 187
Bible, 3–4, 7, 21, 23–24, 34, 35, 40–43, 50, 53–54, 55, 59–60, 63, 65, 70, 80, 89, 92–93, 95–96, 100, 108–109, 116, 134, 147, 170–171, 193, 196–198, 201, 206, 210, 211–212, 216, 218–220, 327, 228, 230, 235
birth, 28, 72–73
birth dates, 82
blasphemy, against Holy Spirit, 199, 201
blood, 168, 180
blood analyses, 82
body, *see* physical body
bones, 168
"born again" religious conversions, 199
bowels, 168, 182, 186, 187

THE EDGAR CAYCE LEGACIES

Among the vast resources which have grown out of the late Edgar Cayce's work are:

The Readings: Available for examination and study at the Association for Research and Enlightenment, Inc., (A.R.E.®) at Virginia Beach, Va., are 14,256 readings consisting of 49,135 pages of verbatim psychic material plus related correspondence. The readings are the clairvoyant discourses given by Cayce while he was in a self-induced hypnotic sleep-state. These discourses were recorded in shorthand and then typed. Copious indexing and cross-indexing make the readings readily accessible for study.

Research and Information: Medical information which flowed through Cayce is being researched and applied by the research divisions of the Edgar Cayce Foundation. Work is also being done with dreams and other aspects of ESP. Much information is disseminated through the A.R.E. Press publications, *A.R.E. News* and *The A.R.E. Journal.* Coordination of a nationwide program of lectures and conferences is in the hands of the Department of Education. A library specializing in psychic literature is available to the public with books on loan to members. An extensive tape library has A.R.E. lectures available for purchase. Resource material has been made available for authors, resulting in the publication of scores of books, booklets and other material.

A.R.E. Study Groups: The Edgar Cayce material is most valuable when worked within an A.R.E. Study Group, the text for which is *A Search for God,* Books I and II. These books are the outcome of eleven years of work by Edgar Cayce with the first A.R.E. group and represent the distillation of wisdom which flowed through him in the trance condition. Hundreds of A.R.E. groups flourish throughout the United States and other countries. Their primary purpose is to assist the members to know their relationship to their Creator and to become channels of love and service to others. The groups are nondenominational and avoid ritual and dogma. There are no dues or fees required to join a group although contributions may be accepted.

Membership: A.R.E. has an open-membership policy which offers attractive benefits.

For more information write A.R.E., Box 595, Virginia Beach, Va. 23451. To obtain information about publications, please direct your query to A.R.E. Press. To obtain information about joining or perhaps starting an A.R.E. Study Group, please direct your letter to the Study Group Department.

ABOUT THE AUTHOR

HERBERT BRUCE PURYEAR, Ph.D. is a trained clinical psychologist who holds a B.A. degree from Stanford University and a Ph.D. from the University of North Carolina. Dr. Puryear serves as Director of Research Services for the Association for Research and Enlightenment (A.R.E.) in Virginia Beach, Virginia. He is the author of *Reflections on the Path* and coauthor of *Meditations and the Mind of Man.* He is also the author of the A.R.E. lesson series, *Covenant,* upon which much of *The Edgar Cayce Primer* is based. Several years ago, Dr. Puryear hosted a nationally televised, twenty-six part series, *Who Is Man?*, an extensive inquiry into parapsychological research.

PSYCHIC WORLD

Here are some of the leading books that delve into the world of the occult—that shed light on the powers of prophecy, of reincarnation and of foretelling the future.

☐	01262	**ALAN OKEN'S COMPLETE ASTROLOGY** by Alan Oken **A Large Format Book**	$9.95
☐	01366	**THE COMPLETE ASTROLOGER** by Parkers **A Large Format Book**	$11.95
☐	20948	**ASTROLOGY FOR THE MILLIONS** by Grant Lewi	$3.50
☐	20511	**EDGAR CAYCE: THE SLEEPING PROPHET** by Jess Stearn	$3.50
☐	20549	**YOGA, YOUTH & REINCARNATION** by Jess Stearn	$2.95
☐	20546	**SETH SPEAKS** by Jane Roberts	$3.95
☐	20550	**THE SETH MATERIAL** by Jane Roberts	$3.50
☐	20446	**YESTERDAY, TODAY, AND FOREVER** by Jeanne Dixon	$3.50
☐	20229	**LINDA GOODMAN'S SUN SIGNS**	$3.95
☐	22560	**THE NATURE OF PERSONAL REALITY** by Jane Roberts	$3.95
☐	20996	**A COMPLETE GUIDE TO THE TAROT** by Eden Gray	$3.25

Buy them at your local bookstore or use this handy coupon for ordering:

Heartwarming Books
of
Faith and Inspiration

☐	22739	**CONFESSIONS OF A HAPPY CHRISTIAN** Zig Ziglar	$2.75
☐	20571	**THE SCREWTAPE LETTERS** C. S. Lewis	$1.95
☐	23069	**A SEVERE MERCY** Sheldon Vanauken	$3.50
☐	20831	**THE GUIDEPOSTS TREASURY OF LOVE**	$2.95
☐	20808	**THREE STEPS FORWARD TWO STEPS BACK** Charles S. Swindoll	$2.50
☐	20564	**MEETING GOD AT EVERY TURN** Catherine Marshall	$2.95
☐	20376	**CROSSROADS** by L. Jaworski/D. Schneider	$2.95
☐	14725	**PILGRIMS REGRESS** C. S. Lewis	$2.50
☐	20299	**MERTON: A BIOGRAPHY**	$3.95
☐	20464	**LOVE AND LIVING** Thomas Merton	$3.50
☐	23069	**A SEVERE MERCY** Sheldon Vanauken	$3.50
☐	20784	**POSITIVE PRAYERS FOR POWER-FILLED LIVING** Robert H. Schuller	$2.50
☐	14732	**HOW CAN I FIND YOU, GOD?** Marjorie Holmes	$2.50
☐	22892	**THE GREATEST MIRACLE IN THE WORLD** Og Mandino	$2.75
☐	22638	**THE GREATEST SECRET IN THE WORLD** Og Mandino	$2.75
☐	14515	**CHRIST COMMISSION** Og Mandino	$2.75
☐	20102	**THE 1980'S COUNTDOWN TO ARMAGEDDON** Hal Lindsey	$2.95
☐	22909	**THE GREATEST SALESMAN IN THE WORLD** Og Mandino	$2.75
☐	14971	**I'VE GOT TO TALK TO SOMEBODY, GOD** Marjorie Holmes	$2.50
☐	22805	**BORN AGAIN** Charles Colson	$3.50
☐	14840	**A GRIEF OBSERVED** C. S. Lewis	$2.50
☐	20727	**LIGHTHOUSE** Eugenia Price	$2.95
☐	22502	**THE LATE GREAT PLANET EARTH** Hal Lindsey	$2.95

Buy them at your local bookstore or use this handy coupon for ordering:

Bantam Books, Inc., Dept. HF, 414 East Golf Road, Des Plaines, Ill. 60016

Please send me the books I have checked above. I am enclosing $_____
(please add $1.00 to cover postage and handling). Send check or money order
—no cash or C.O.D.'s please.

Mr/Mrs/Miss_____

Address_____

City_____ State/Zip_____

HF—8/82

Please allow four to six weeks for delivery. This offer expires 2/83.

We Deliver!
And So Do These Bestsellers.